DRACULA

Victor G Ambrus

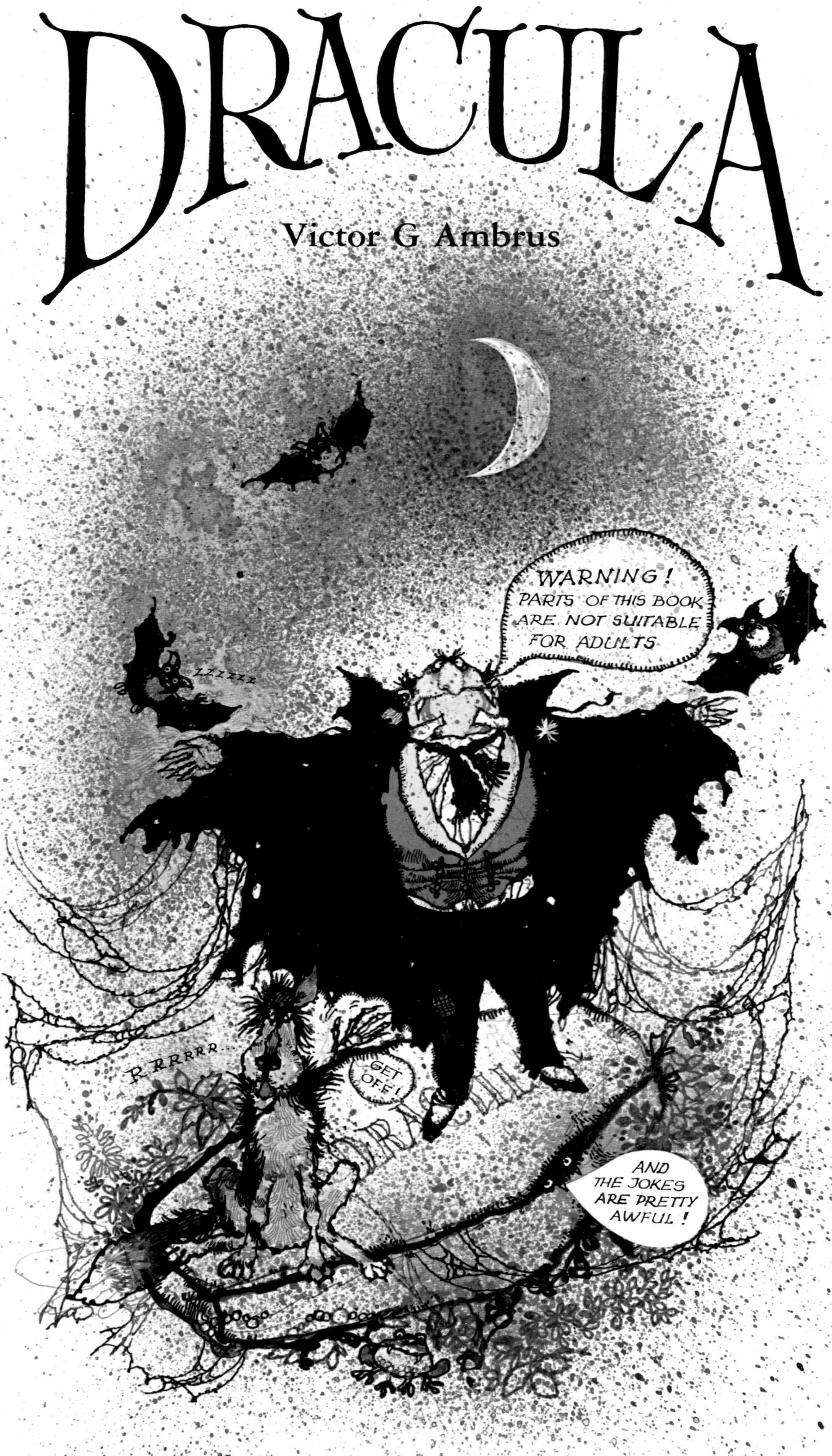
WARNING!
PARTS OF THIS BOOK
ARE NOT SUITABLE
FOR ADULTS
ZZZZZZ
R-RRRRR...
GET OFF!
AND
THE JOKES
ARE PRETTY
AWFUL!

Oxford New York Toronto Melbourne
OXFORD UNIVERSITY PRESS 1980

Oxford University Press, Walton Street, Oxford OX2 6DP
OXFORD LONDON GLASGOW
NEW YORK TORONTO MELBOURNE WELLINGTON
KUALA LUMPUR SINGAPORE HONG KONG TOKYO
DELHI BOMBAY CALCUTTA MADRAS KARACHI
NAIROBI DAR ES SALAAM CAPE TOWN

British Library Cataloguing in Publication Data

Ambrus, Victor
Dracula.
I. Title
741.5'9439   PN6790.H/   80-41021

PHOTOTYPESET BY TRADESPOOLS LIMITED, FROME, SOMERSET
PRINTED IN GREAT BRITAIN BY WILLIAM CLOWES (BECCLES) LIMITED

ISBN 0-19-279746-8

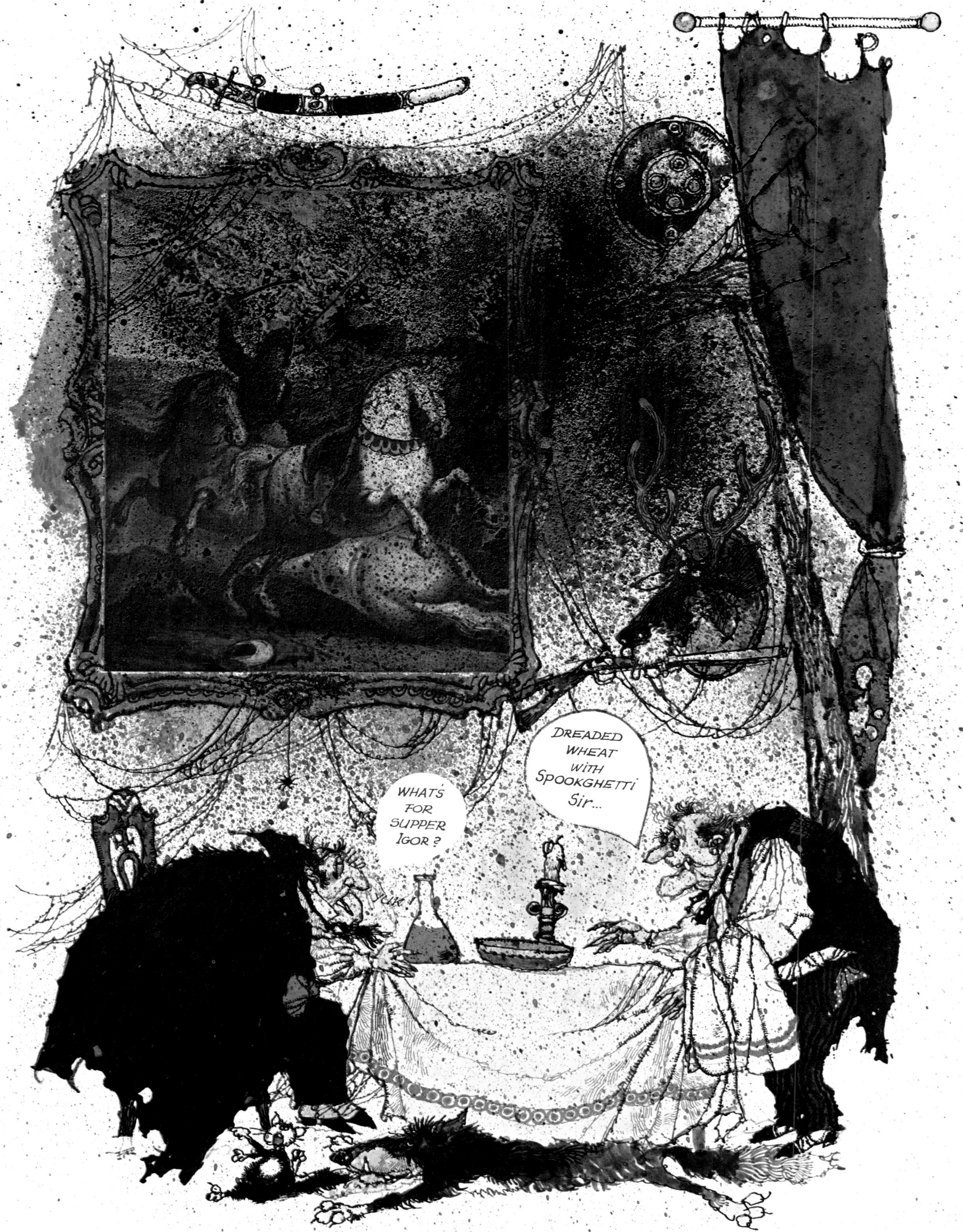
WHAT'S FOR SUPPER IGOR ?
DREADED WHEAT WITH SPOOKGHETTI Sir...
YUK!

Deep in Transylvania, far away in the mountains, lives Count Dracula in his once-proud home, Castle Drac. But, alas, dust and cobwebs cover the beautiful pictures.

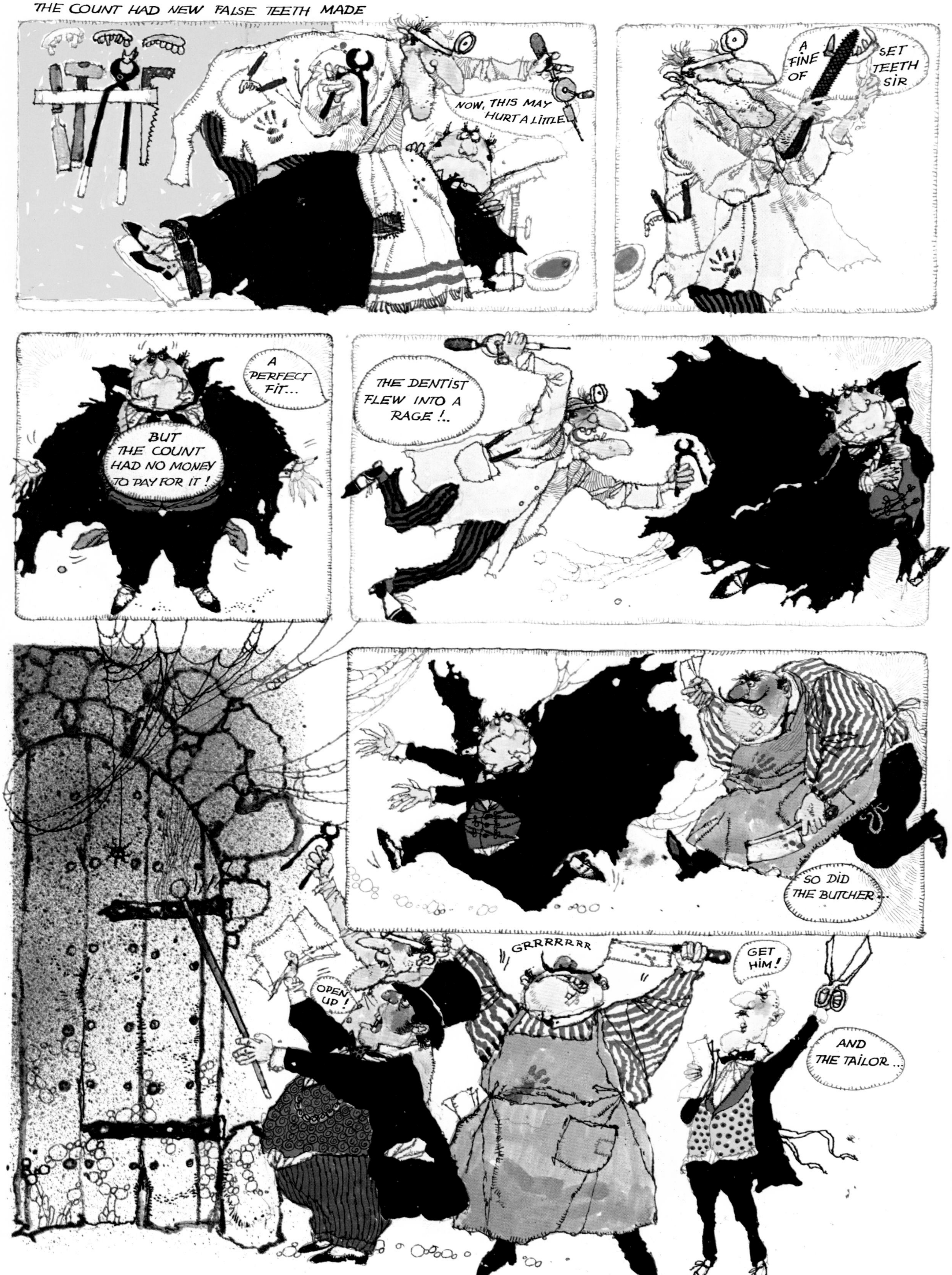
THE COUNT HAD NEW FALSE TEETH MADE
NOW, THIS MAY HURT A LITTLE
A FINE SET OF TEETH SIR
A PERFECT FIT...
BUT THE COUNT HAD NO MONEY TO PAY FOR IT!
THE DENTIST FLEW INTO A RAGE!..
SO DID THE BUTCHER...
OPEN UP!
GRRRRRRRR
GET HIM!
AND THE TAILOR...

Count Dracula is broke. The Bank Manager, the Butcher, the Tailor, and the Dentist all want their bills paid.

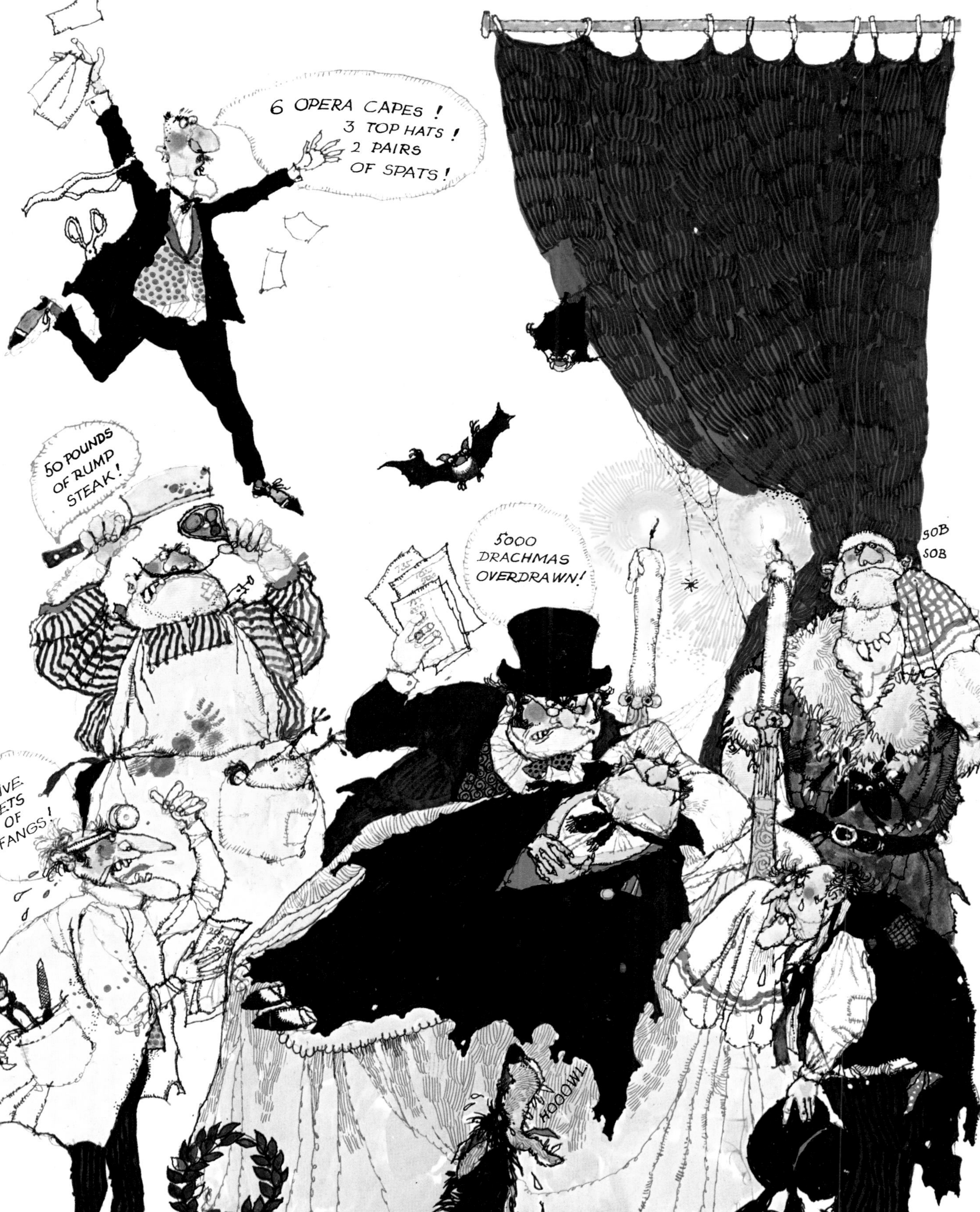
6 OPERA CAPES !
3 TOP HATS !
2 PAIRS
OF SPATS !
50 POUNDS
OF RUMP
STEAK !
5000
DRACHMAS
OVERDRAWN !
SOB
SOB
FIVE
SETS
OF
FANGS !
HOOOWL

And so the poor Count has to pretend to be dead, while all around servants mourn and the creditors rage.

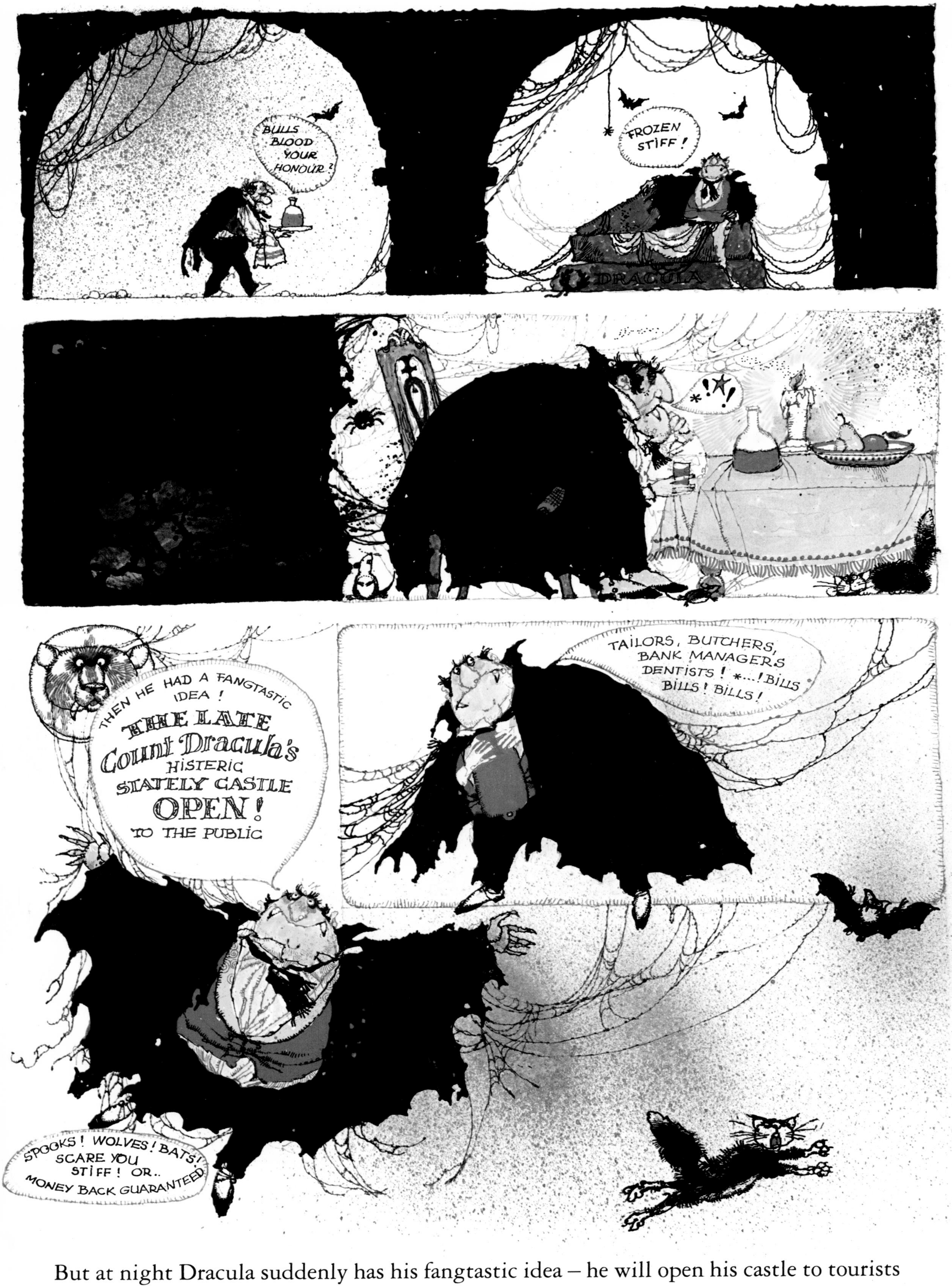

BULLS BLOOD YOUR HONOUR?
FROZEN STIFF!
DRACULA
THEN HE HAD A FANGTASTIC IDEA!
THE LATE Count Dracula's HISTERIC STATELY CASTLE OPEN! TO THE PUBLIC
TAILORS, BUTCHERS, BANK MANAGERS DENTISTS! *...! BILLS BILLS! BILLS!
SPOOKS! WOLVES! BATS! SCARE YOU STIFF! OR.. MONEY BACK GUARANTEED

But at night Dracula suddenly has his fangtastic idea – he will open his castle to tourists and make lots of money.

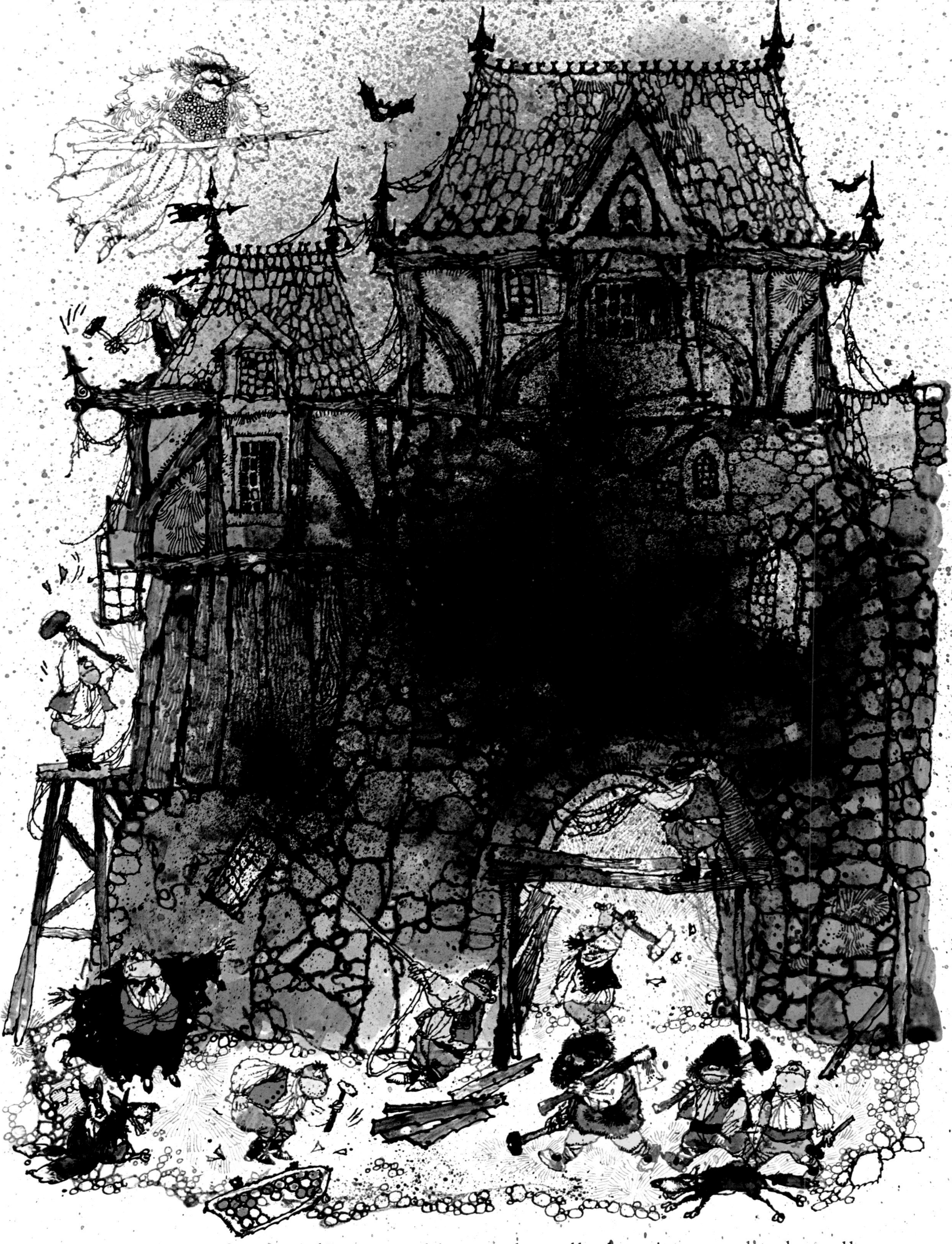

Next day teams of serfs are busy, smashing up the walls, hanging up cobwebs – all to make the castle more horrible than ever.

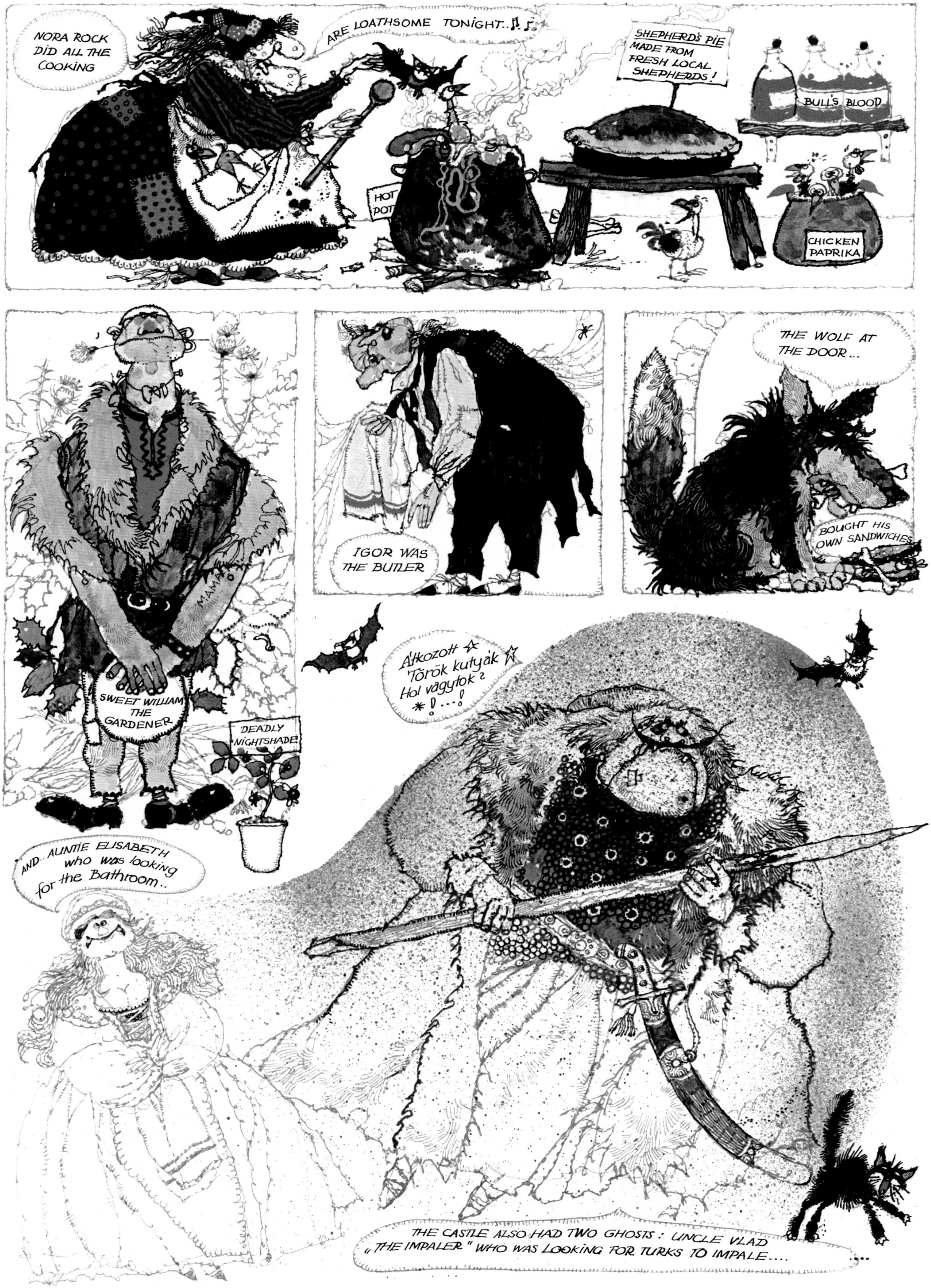
NORA ROCK DID ALL THE COOKING
ARE LOATHSOME TONIGHT..
SHEPHERD'S PIE MADE FROM FRESH LOCAL SHEPHERDS!
BULL'S BLOOD
HOT POT
CHICKEN PAPRIKA
MAMA
SWEET WILLIAM THE GARDENER
DEADLY NIGHTSHADE
IGOR WAS THE BUTLER
THE WOLF AT THE DOOR...
BOUGHT HIS OWN SANDWICHES
Átkozott Török kutyák Hol vagytok? *!...!
AND.. AUNTIE ELISABETH who was looking for the Bathroom..
THE CASTLE ALSO HAD TWO GHOSTS: UNCLE VLAD „THE IMPALER" WHO WAS LOOKING FOR TURKS TO IMPALE....

Everyone gets ready for the grand opening.

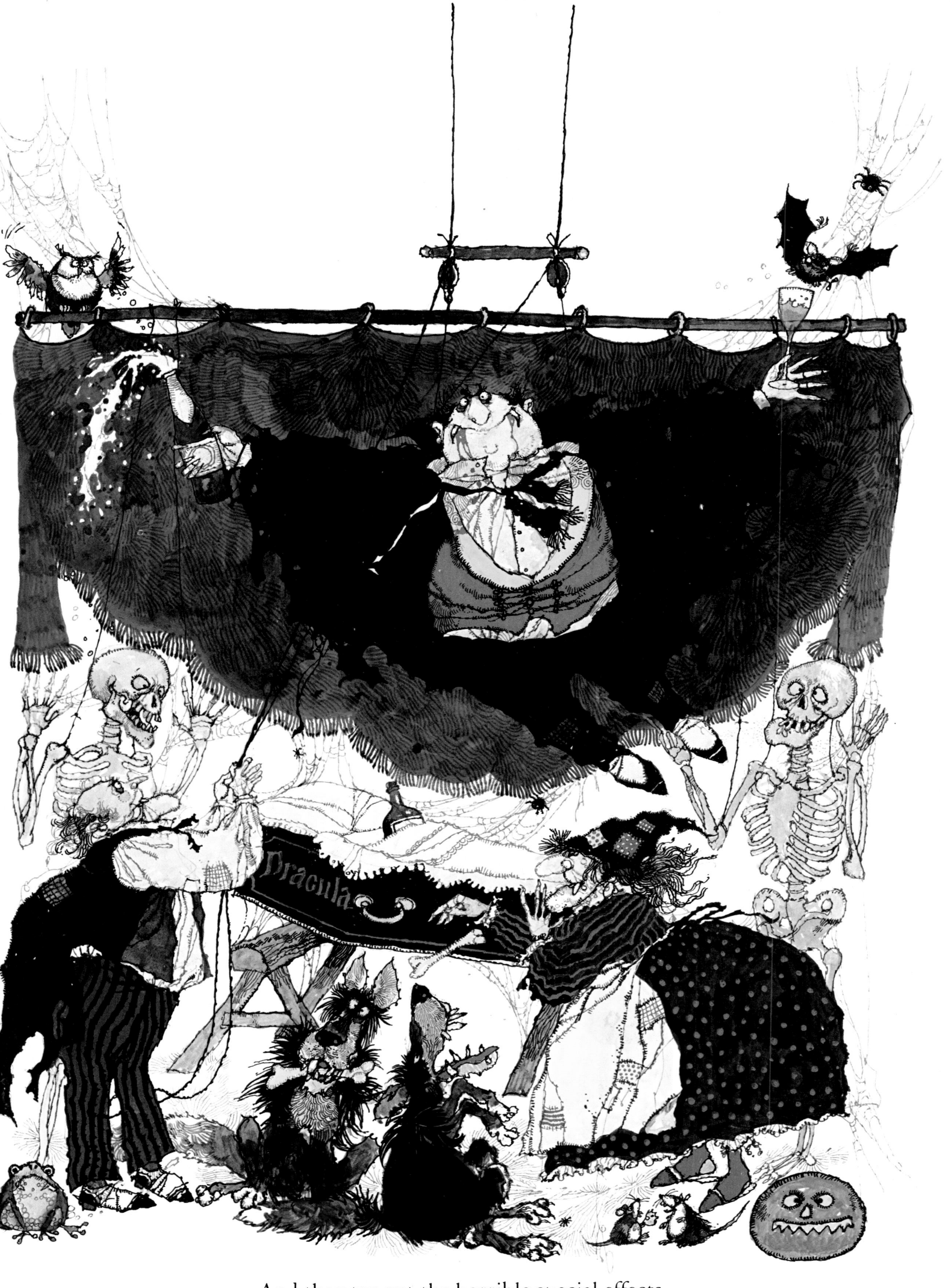
Dracula

And they try out the horrible special effects.

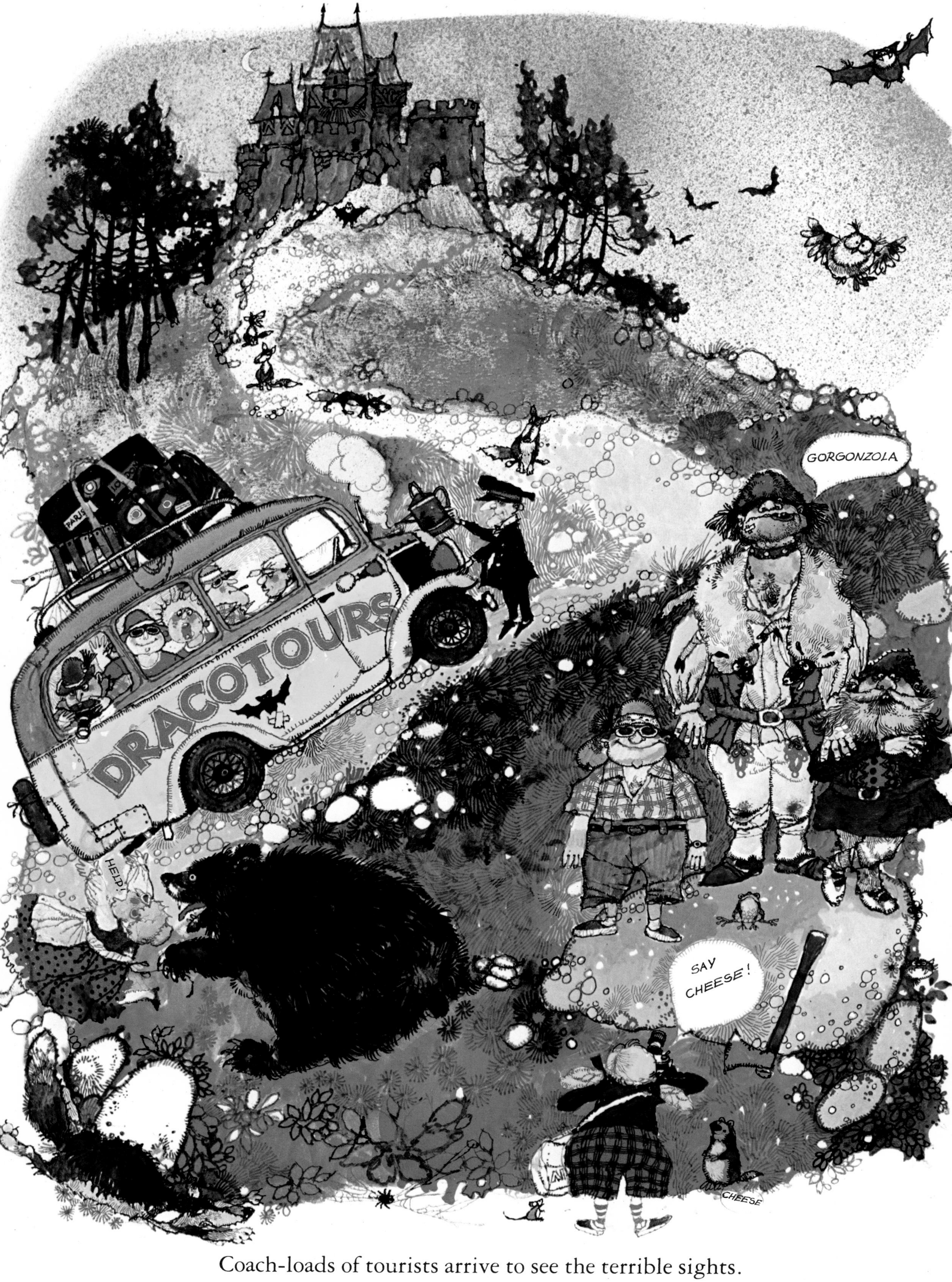
PARIS
DRACOTOURS
GORGONZOLA
HELP!
SAY CHEESE!
CHEESE

Coach-loads of tourists arrive to see the terrible sights.

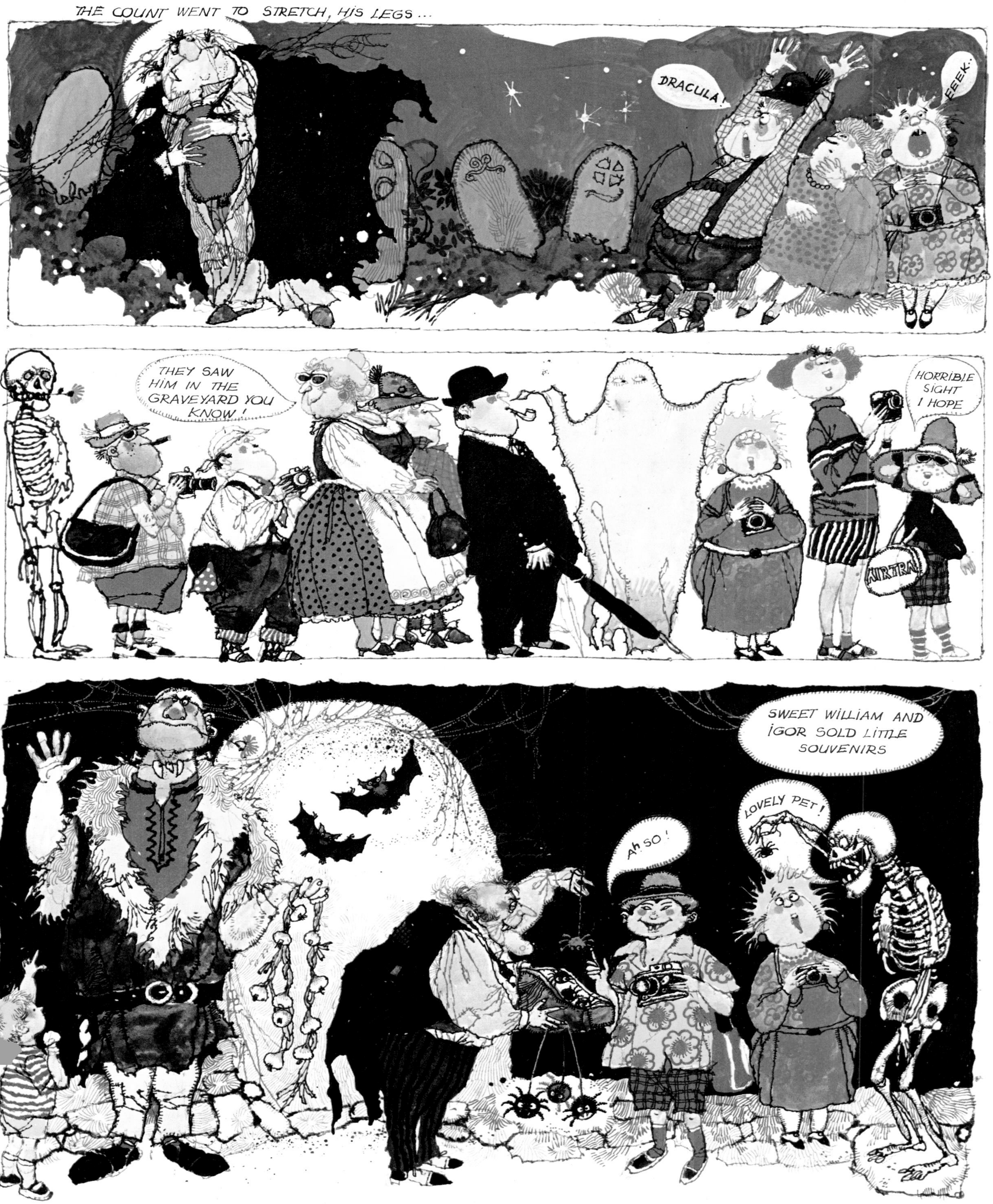
THE COUNT WENT TO STRETCH HIS LEGS...
DRACULA!
EEEK!
THEY SAW HIM IN THE GRAVEYARD YOU KNOW!
HORRIBLE SIGHT I HOPE
SWEET WILLIAM AND IGOR SOLD LITTLE SOUVENIRS
LOVELY PET!
Ah SO!

They join the terrible queue.

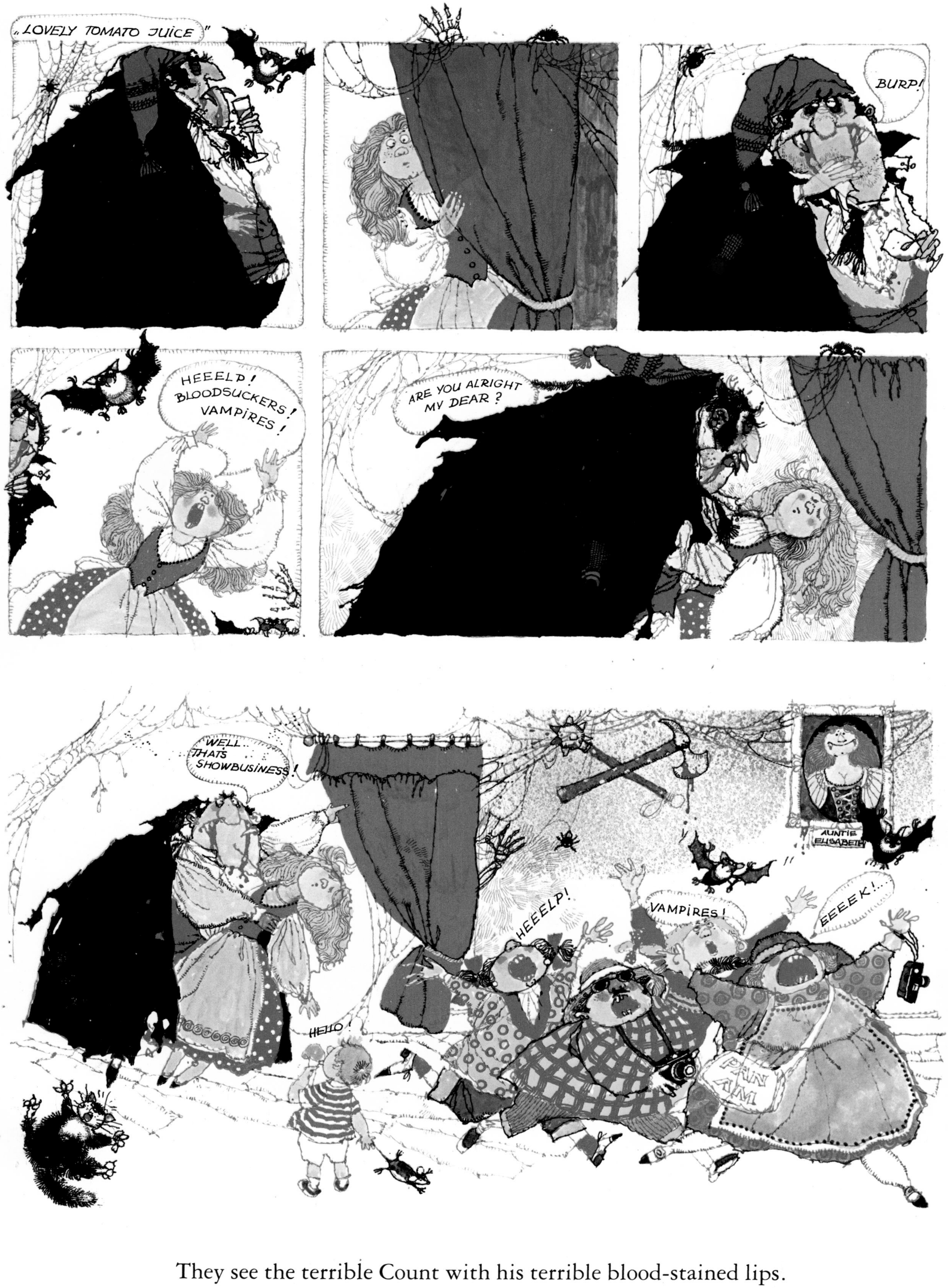
„LOVELY TOMATO JUICE"
BURP!
HEEELP! BLOODSUCKERS! VAMPIRES!
ARE YOU ALRIGHT MY DEAR?
WELL.. THATS SHOWBUSINESS!
AUNTIE ELISABETH
HEEELP!
VAMPIRES!
EEEEK!...
HELLO!
PAN AM

They see the terrible Count with his terrible blood-stained lips.

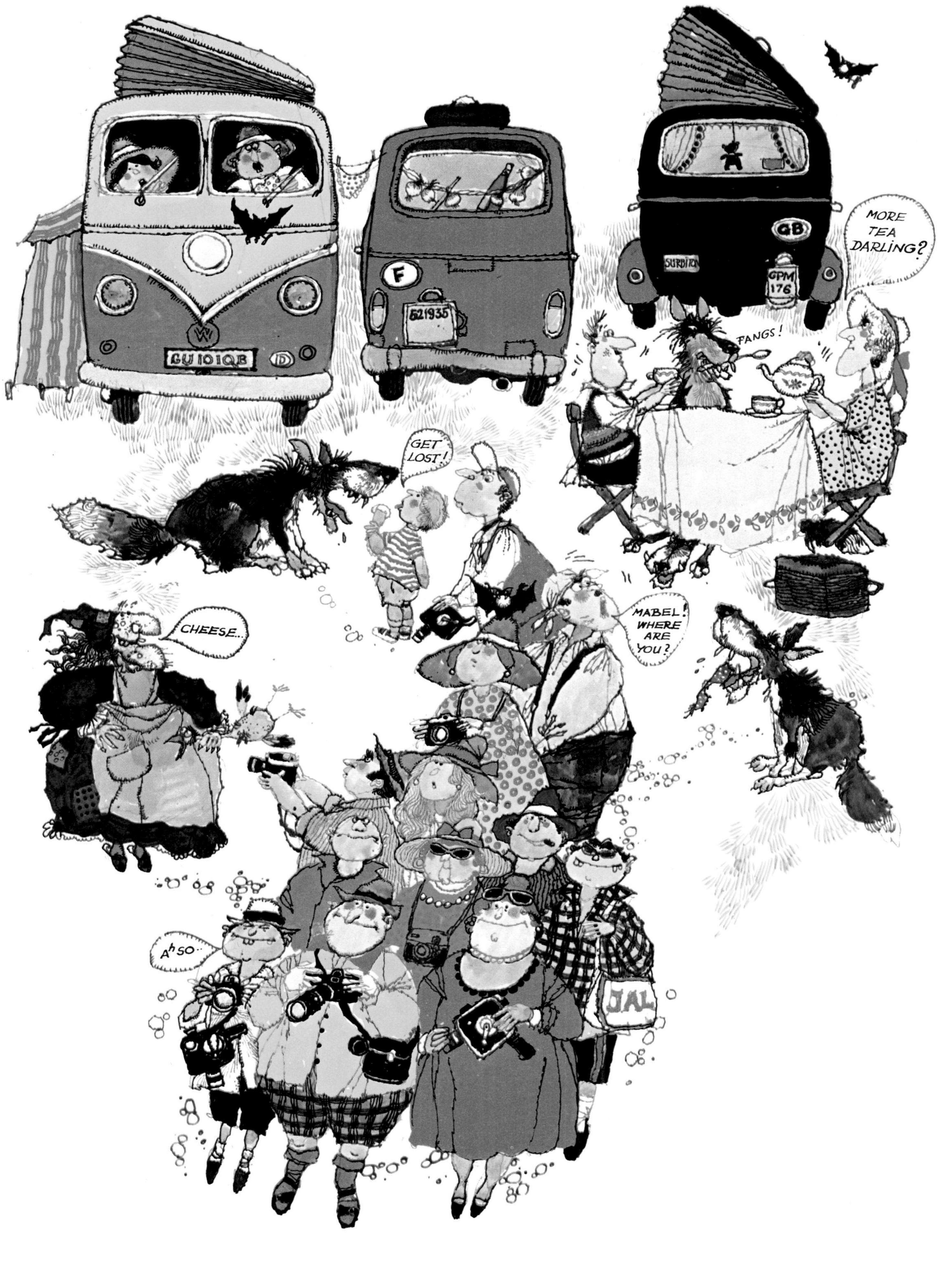
F
521935
GB
GPM 176
MORE TEA DARLING?
FANGS!
GET LOST!
CHEESE...
MABEL! WHERE ARE YOU?
Ah SO...
JAL

The wolves play with the tourists in the car-park.

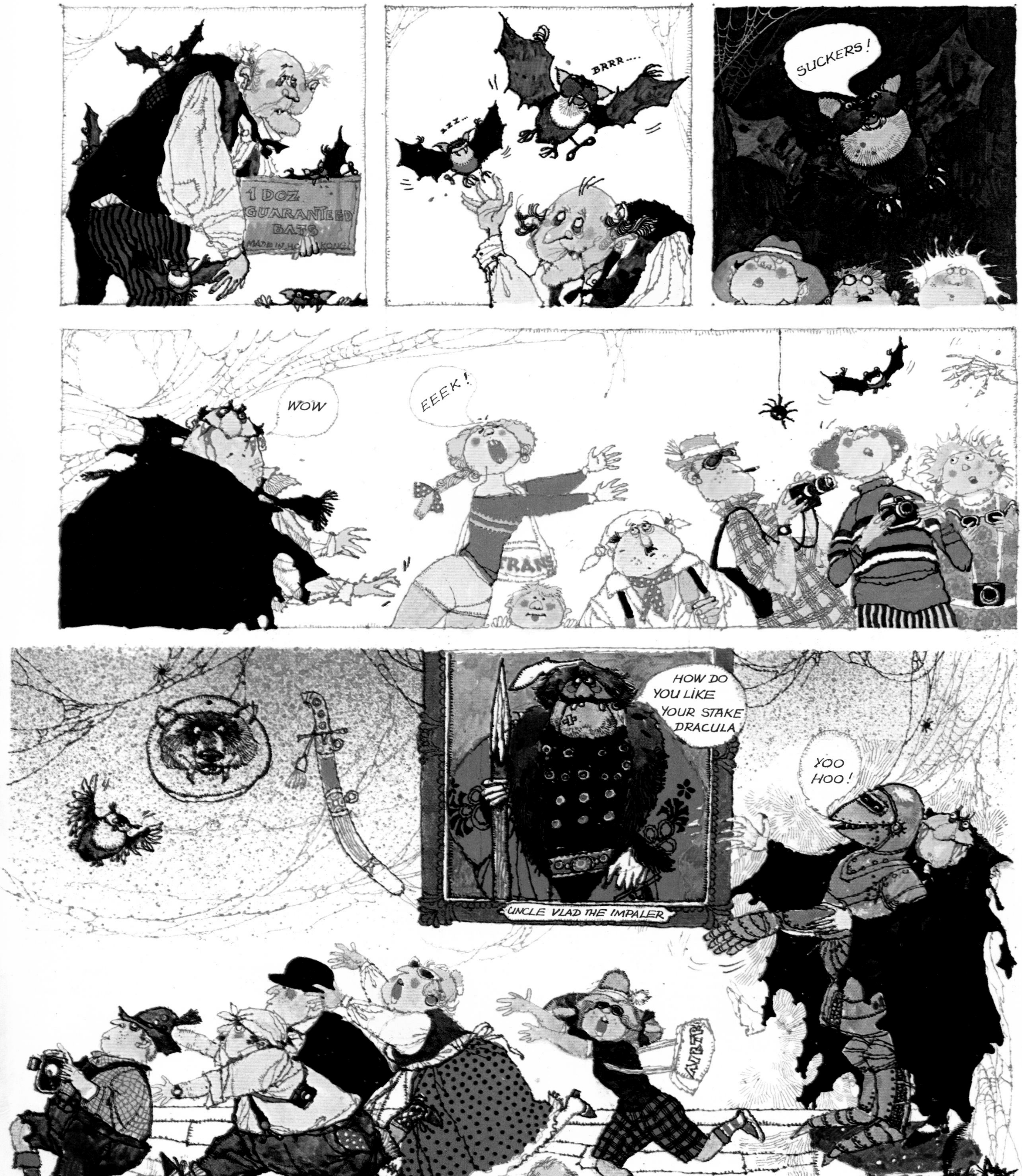
1 DOZ
GUARANTEED
BATS
zzz...
BRRR....
SUCKERS!
WOW
EEEK!
TRANS
HOW DO YOU LIKE YOUR STAKE DRACULA
YOO HOO!
UNCLE VLAD THE IMPALER

Igor and the Count think up new games for the tourists.

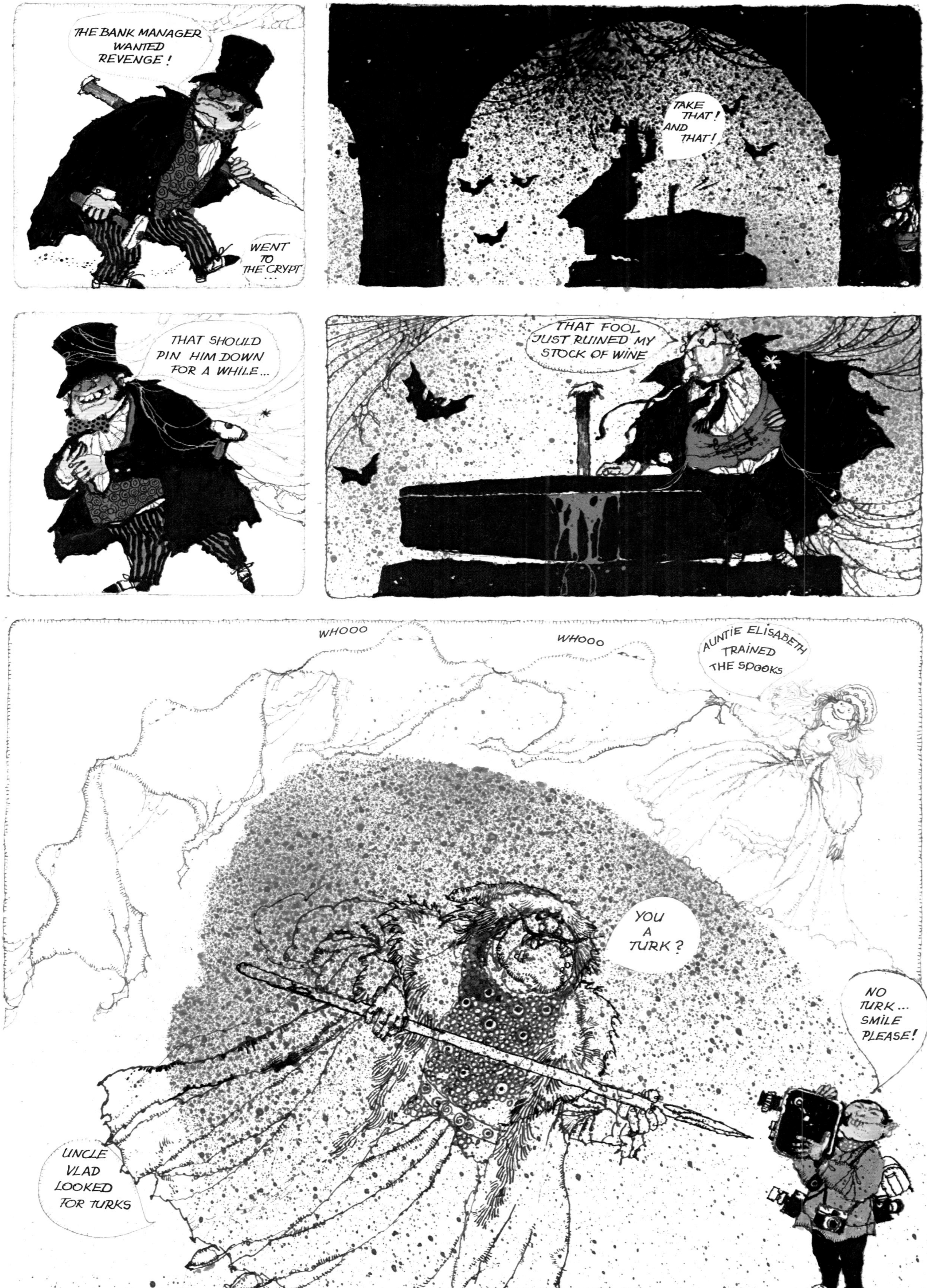
THE BANK MANAGER WANTED REVENGE!
WENT TO THE CRYPT ...
TAKE THAT! AND THAT!
THAT SHOULD PIN HIM DOWN FOR A WHILE...
THAT FOOL JUST RUINED MY STOCK OF WINE
WHOOO
WHOOO
AUNTIE ELISABETH TRAINED THE SPOOKS
YOU A TURK?
NO TURK... SMILE PLEASE!
UNCLE VLAD LOOKED FOR TURKS

But the Bank Manager, not satisfied, seeks revenge.

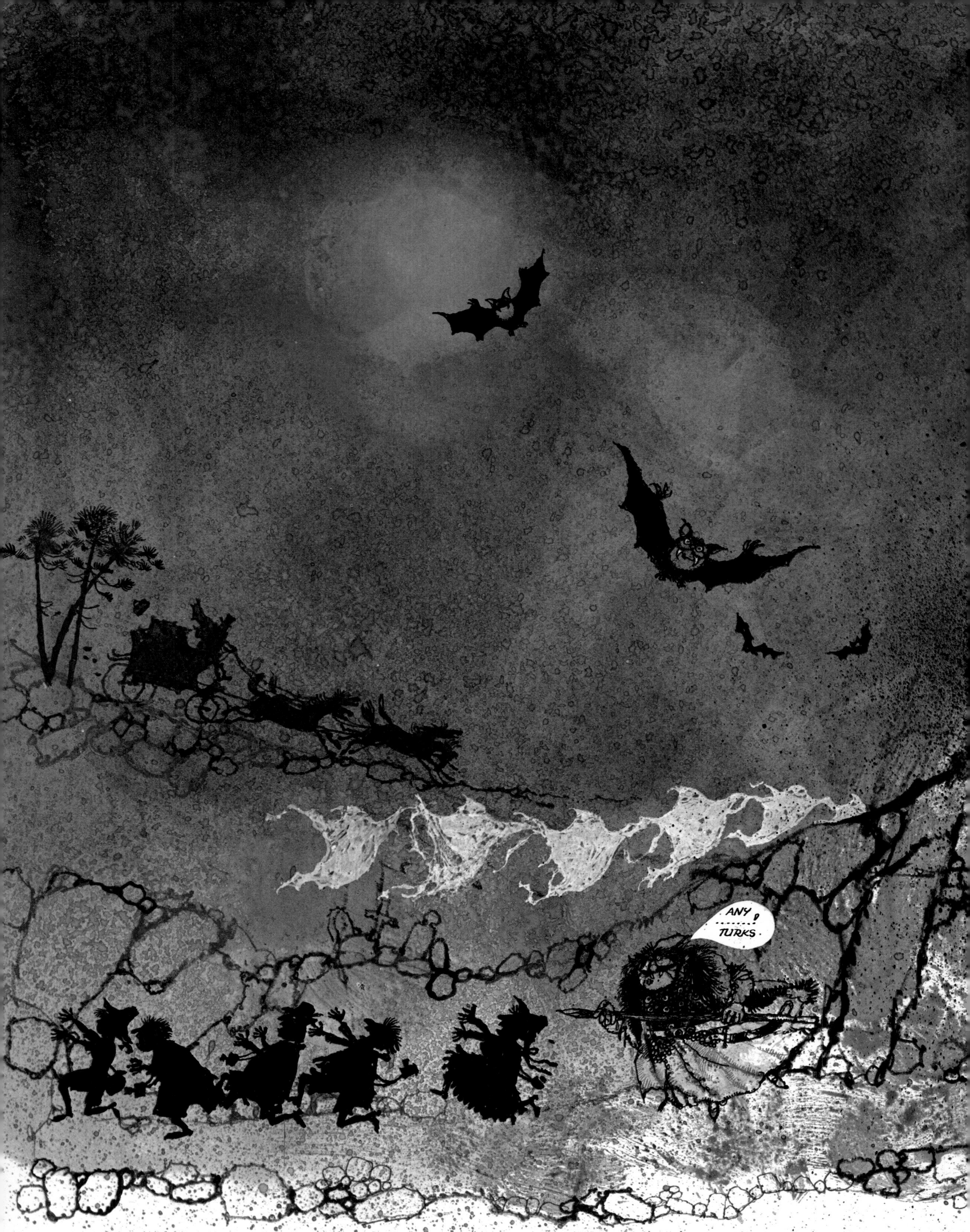
ANY TURKS

When night falls, Uncle Vlad says good-bye to the tourists, and Dracula rises from his coffin to count the day's takings.

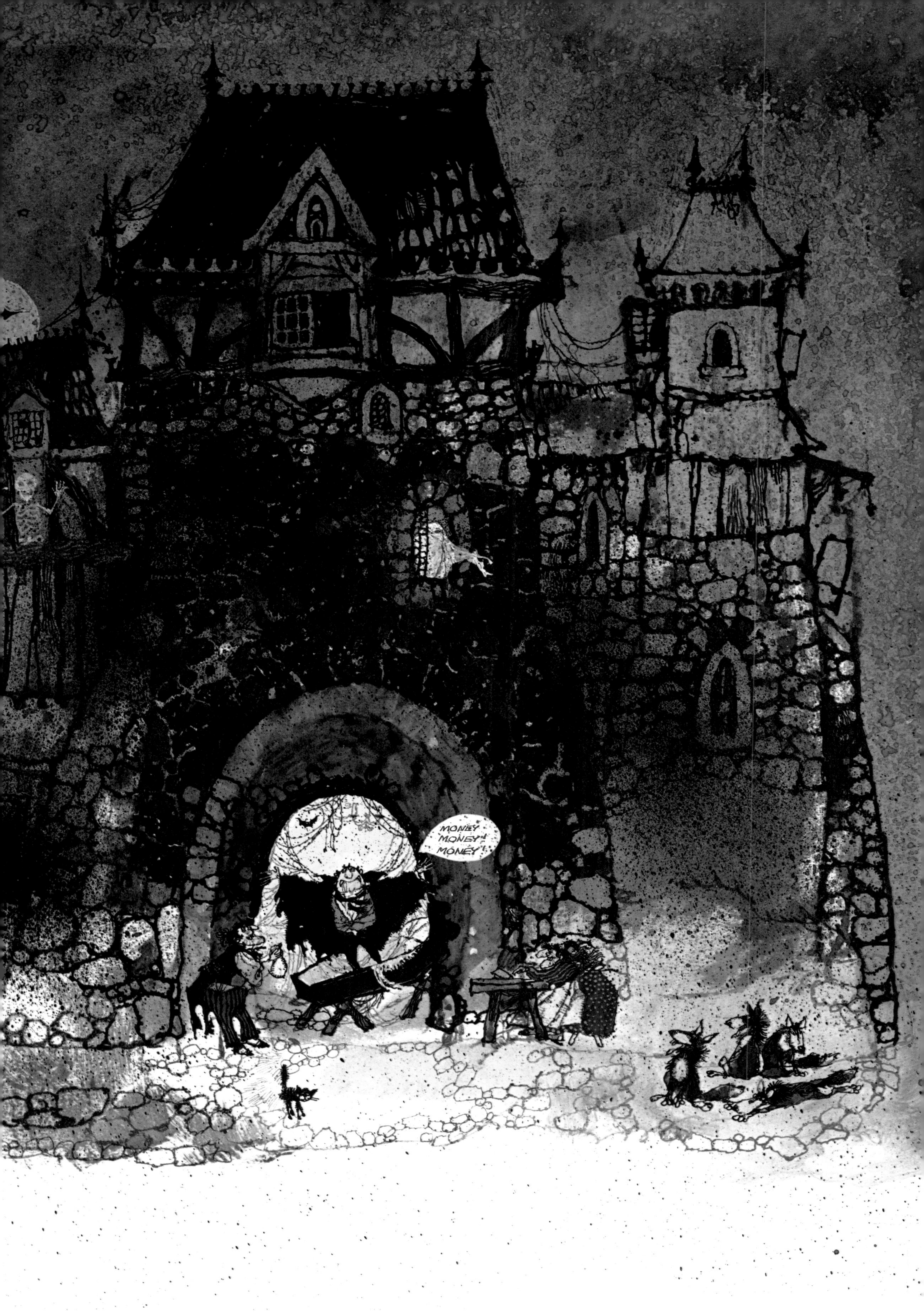
MONEY
MONEY!
MONEY!

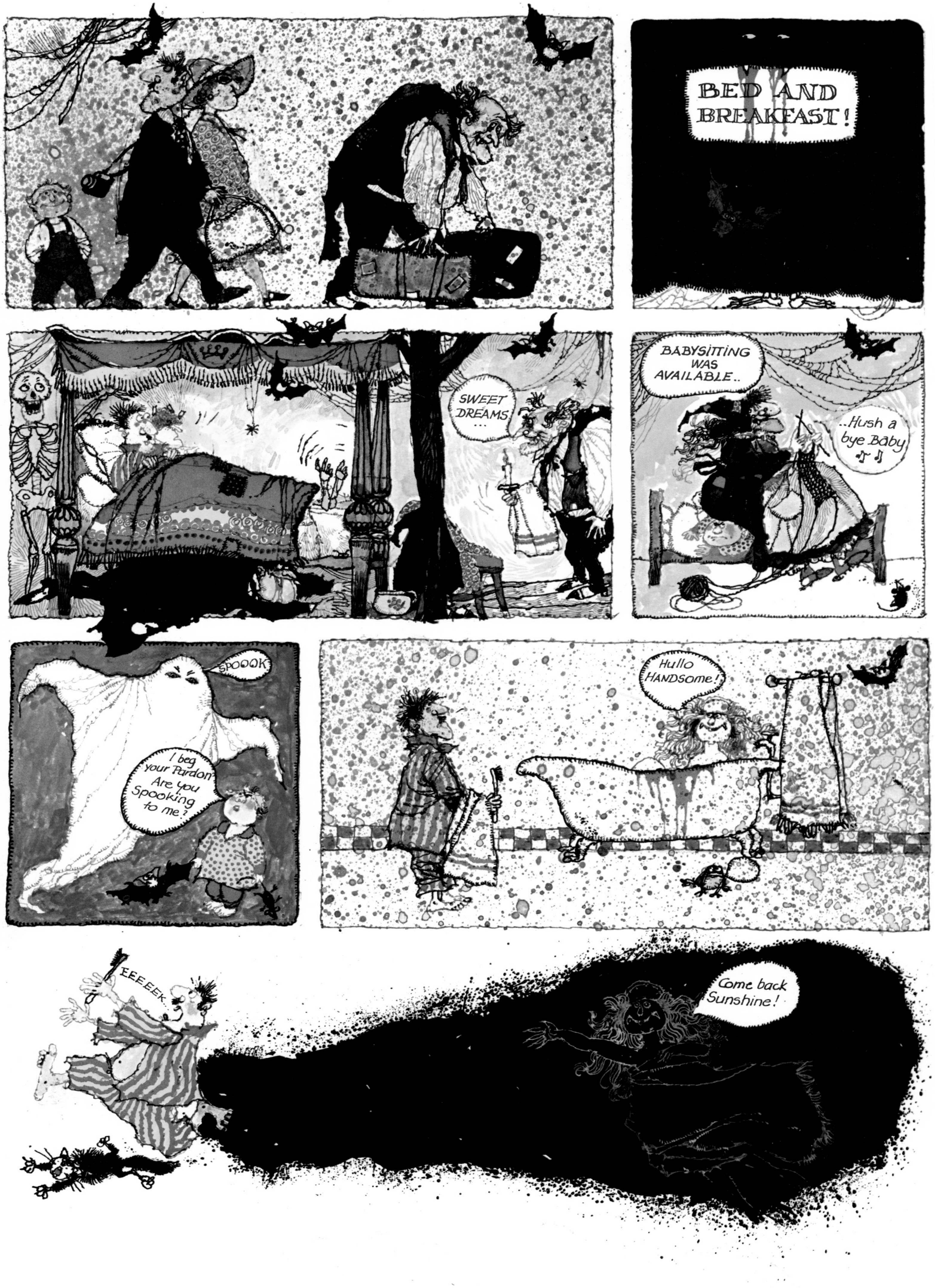
BED AND BREAKFAST!
SWEET DREAMS ...
BABYSITTING WAS AVAILABLE..
..Hush a bye Baby
SPOOOK
I beg your Pardon? Are you Spooking to me?
Hullo HANDSOME!
EEEEEK
Come back Sunshine!

If you are brave,
you can stay the night.
Igor will look after you.

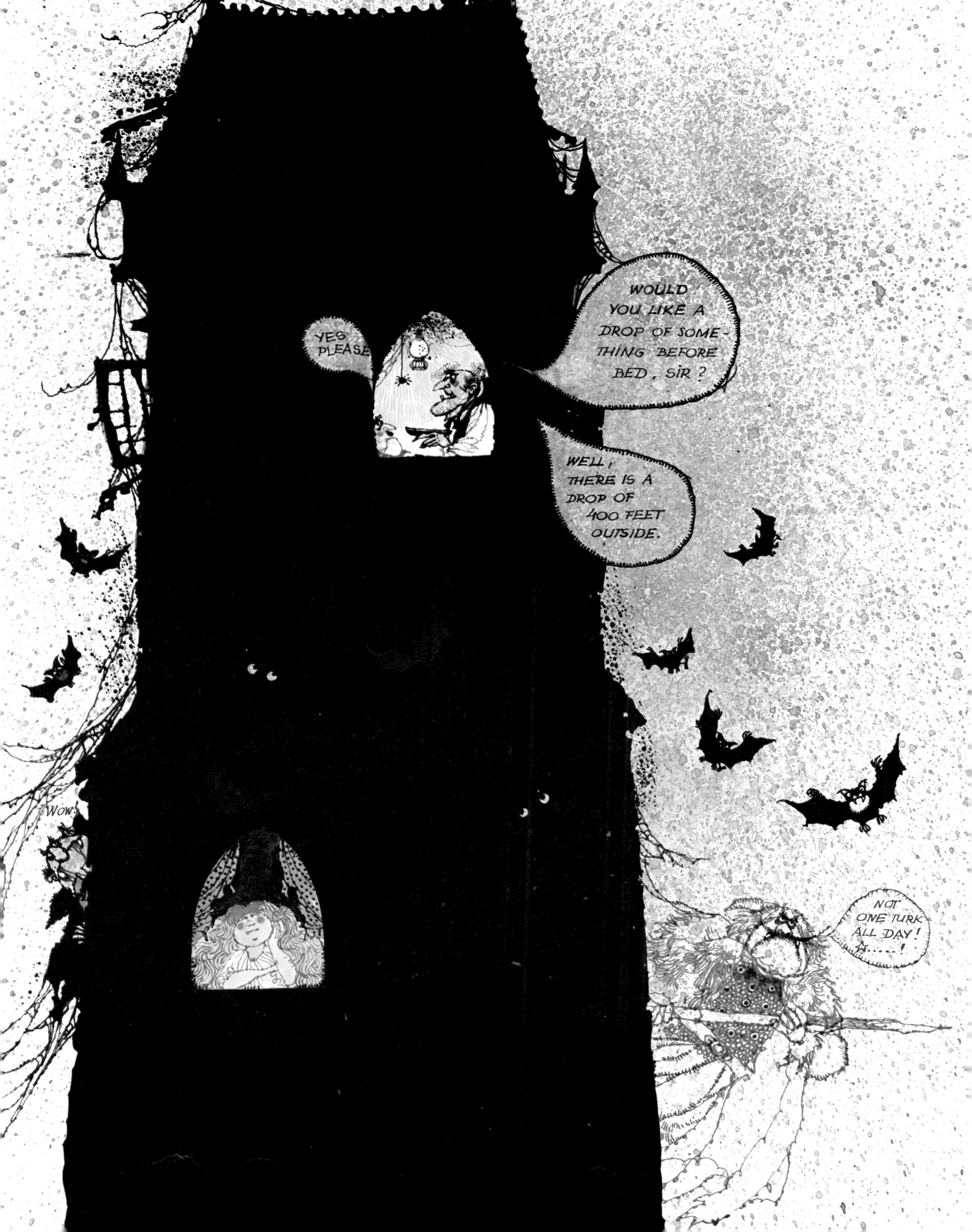
YES PLEASE
WOULD YOU LIKE A DROP OF SOMETHING BEFORE BED, SIR?
WELL, THERE IS A DROP OF 400 FEET OUTSIDE.
Wow!
NOT ONE TURK ALL DAY! ☆.....!

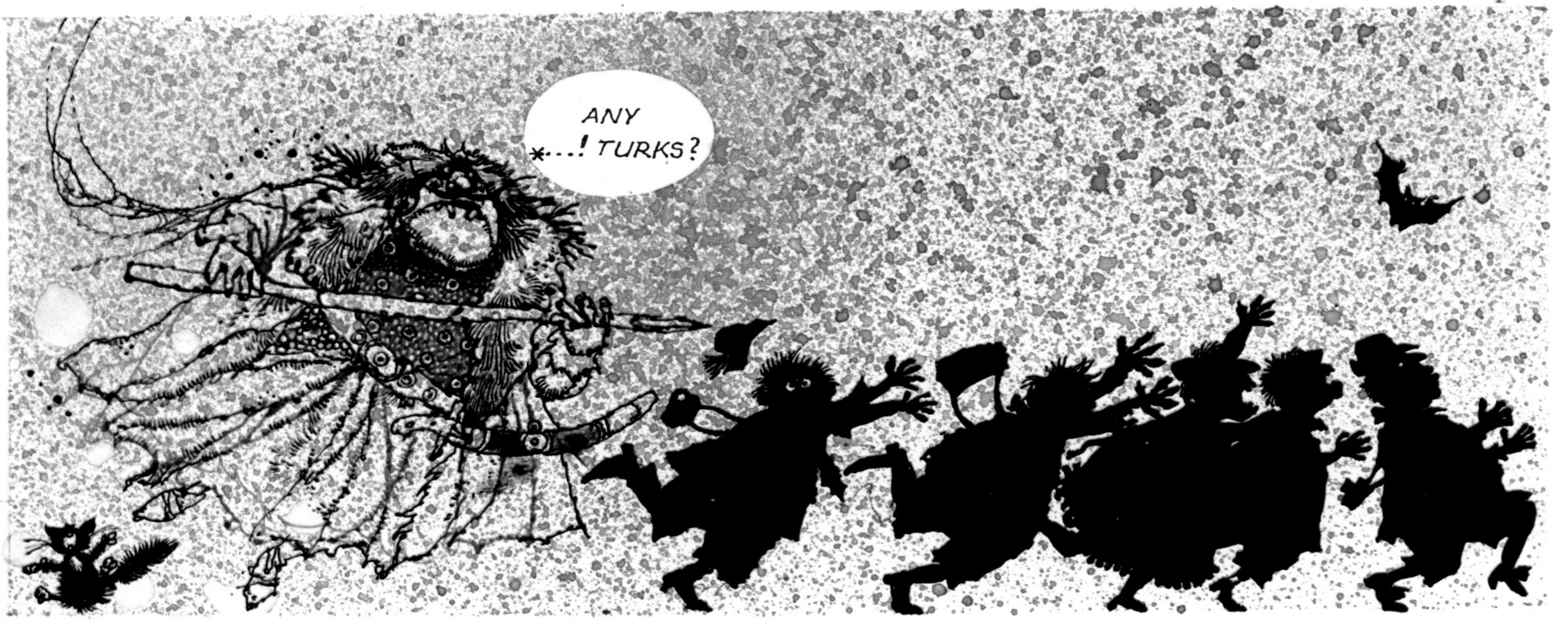
ANY *...! TURKS?

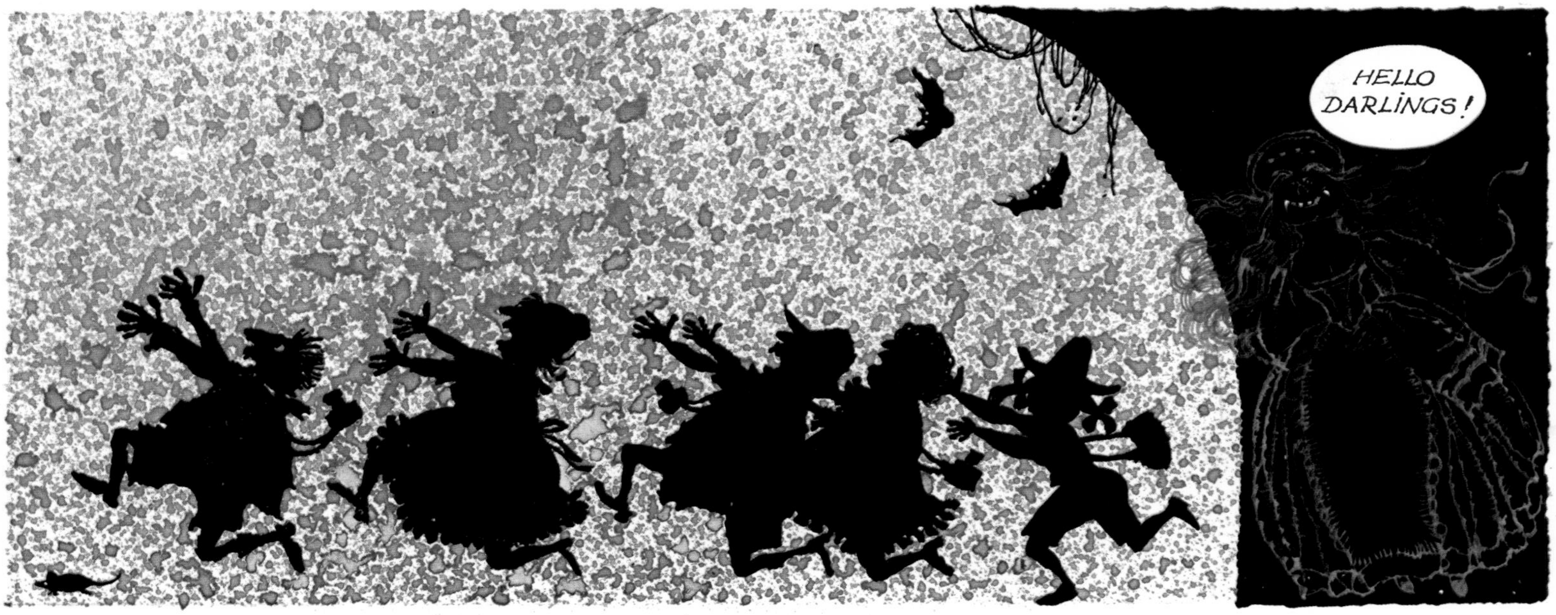
HELLO DARLINGS!

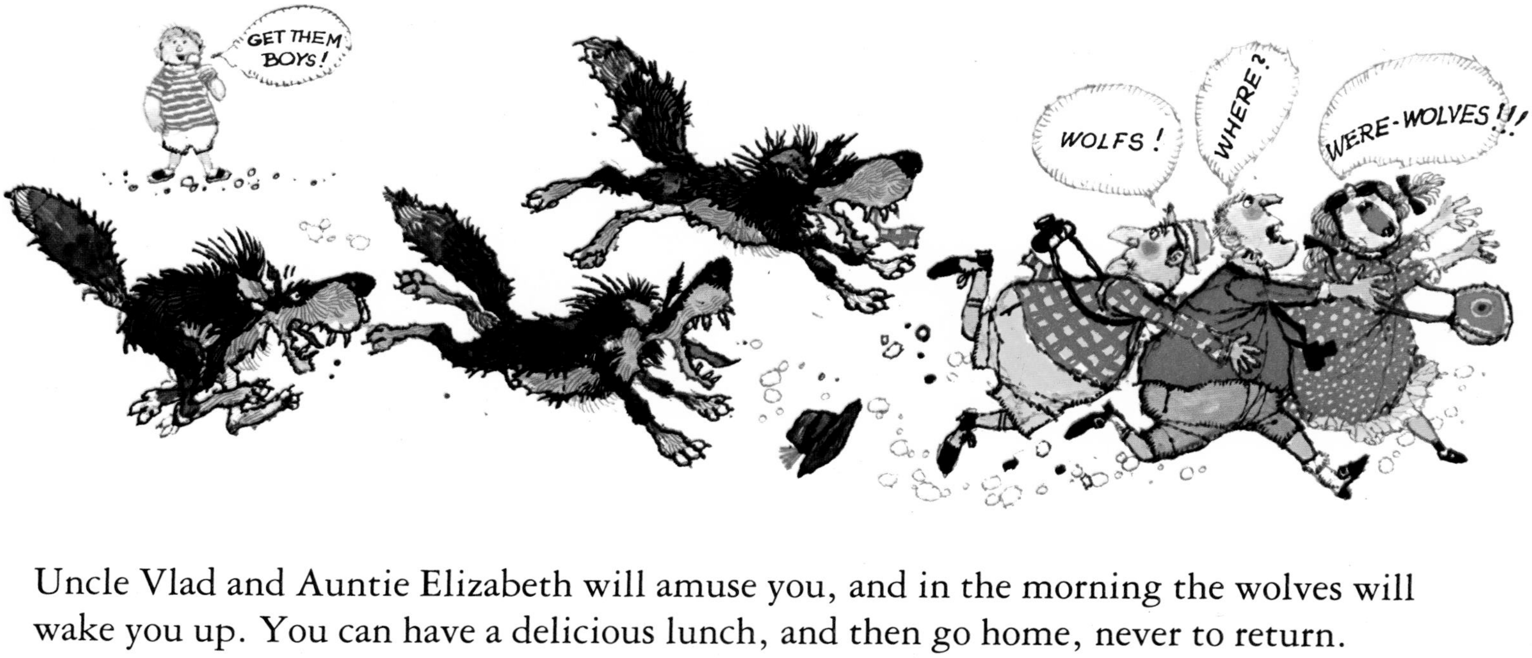
GET THEM BOYS!
WOLFS!
WHERE?
WERE-WOLVES!!!

Uncle Vlad and Auntie Elizabeth will amuse you, and in the morning the wolves will wake you up. You can have a delicious lunch, and then go home, never to return.

AFTER A TOUR OF CASTLE DRAC...

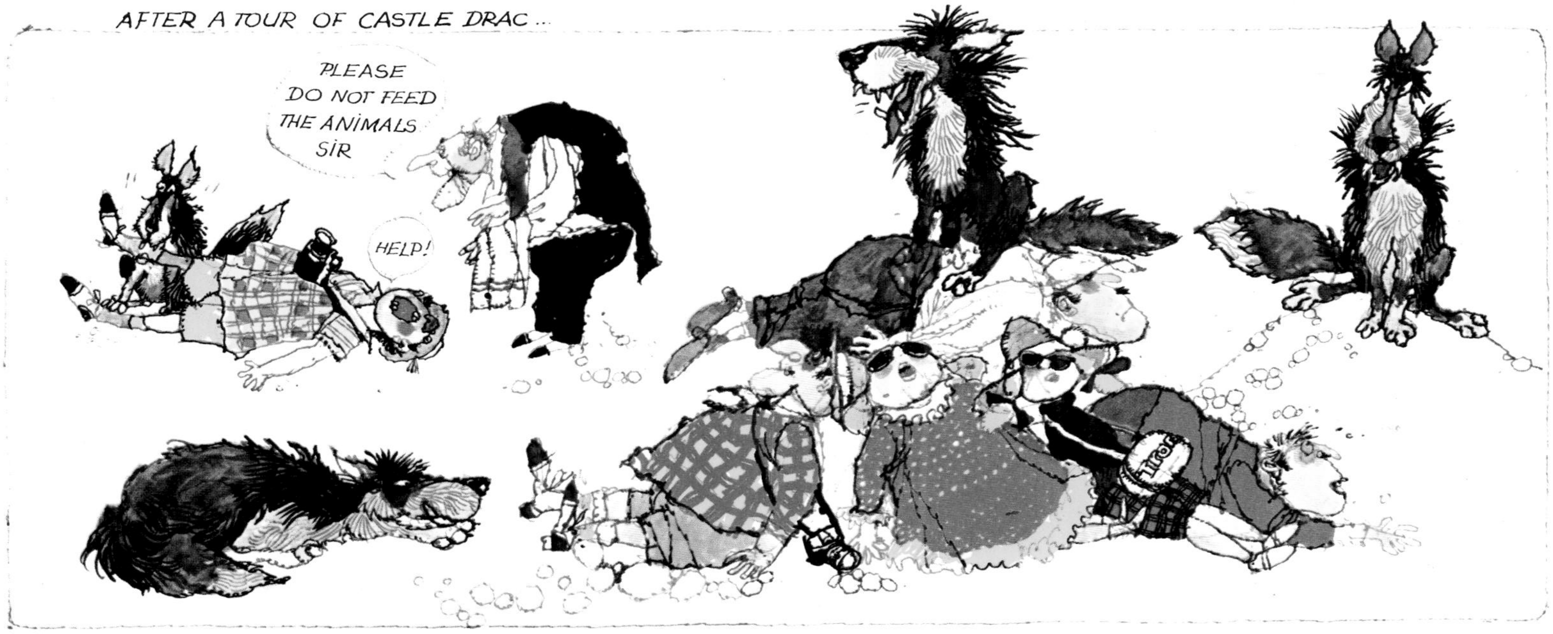
PLEASE DO NOT FEED THE ANIMALS SIR
HELP!

NORA ROCK SERVED REFRESHMENTS!

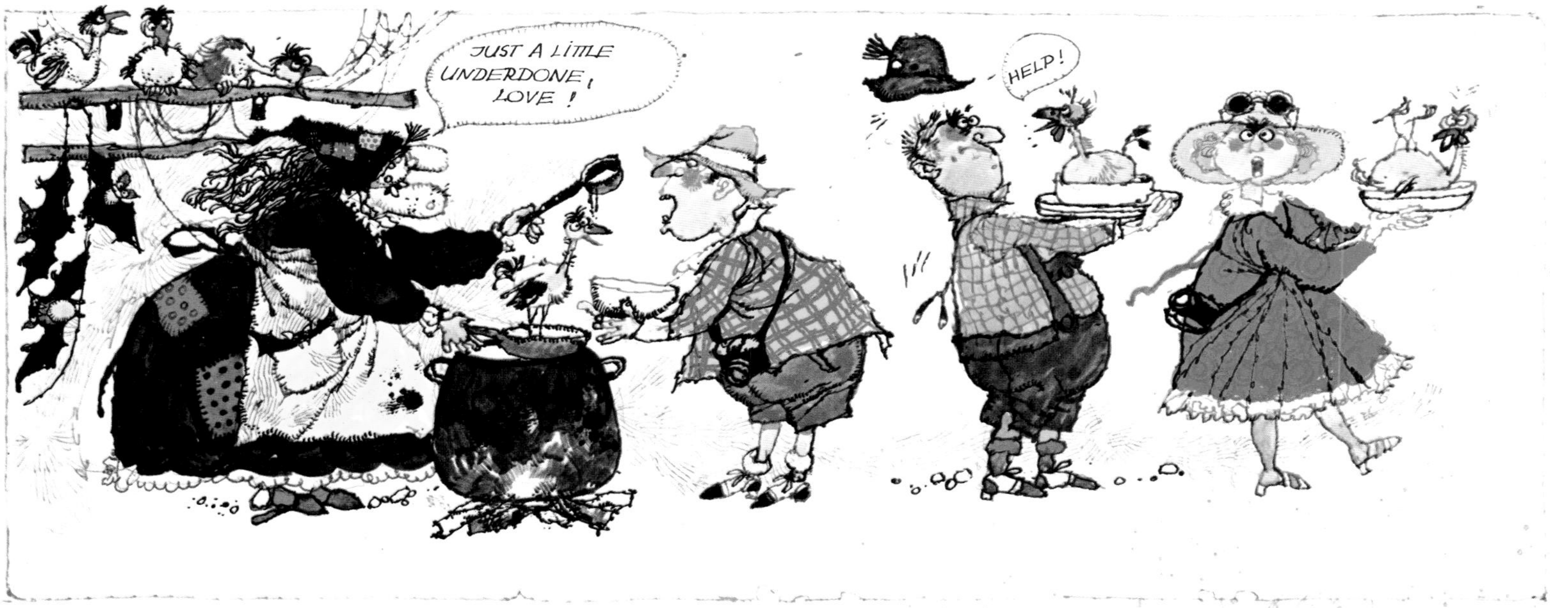
JUST A LITTLE UNDERDONE, LOVE!
HELP!

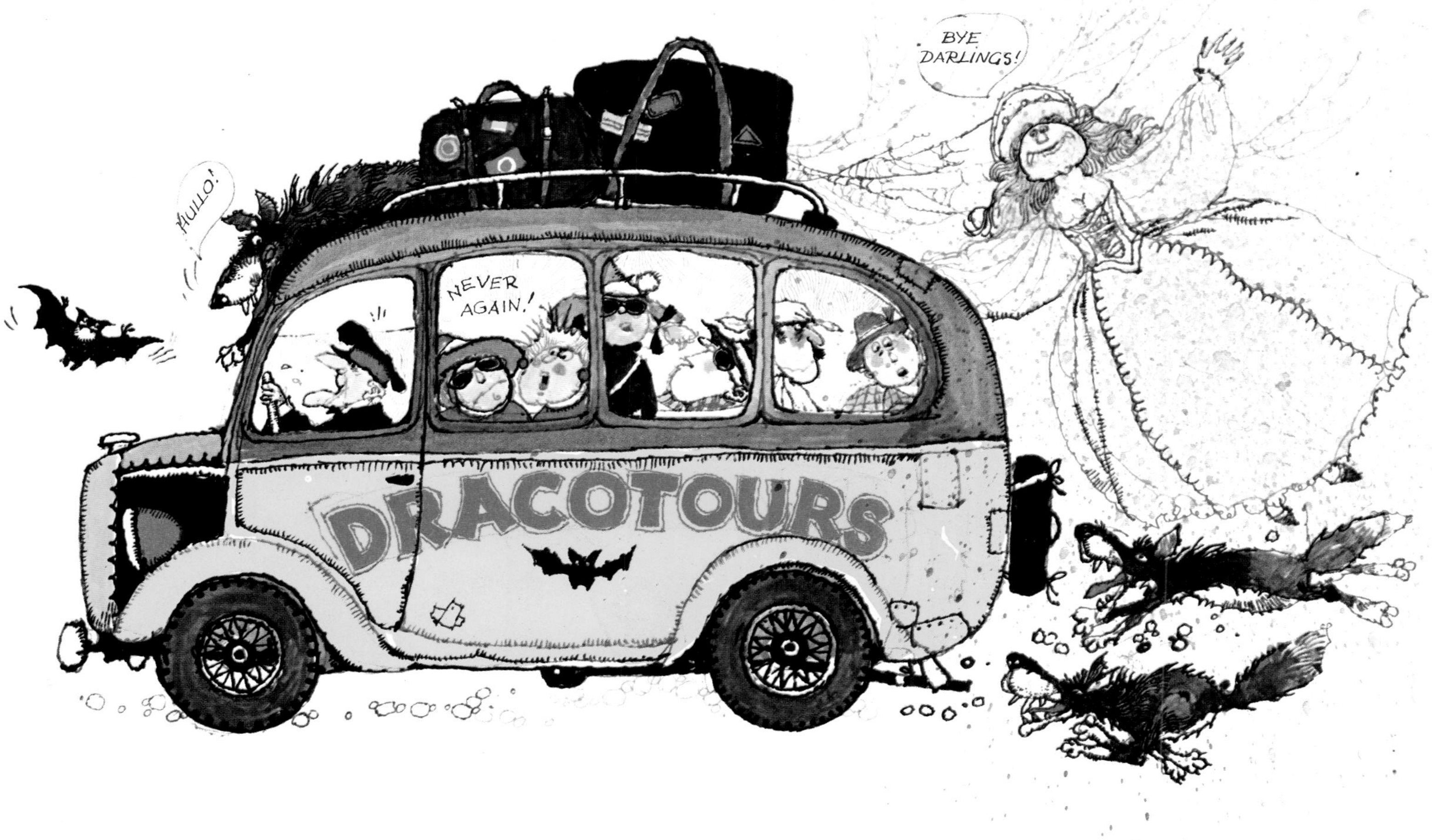
HULLO!
NEVER AGAIN!
BYE DARLINGS!
DRACOTOURS

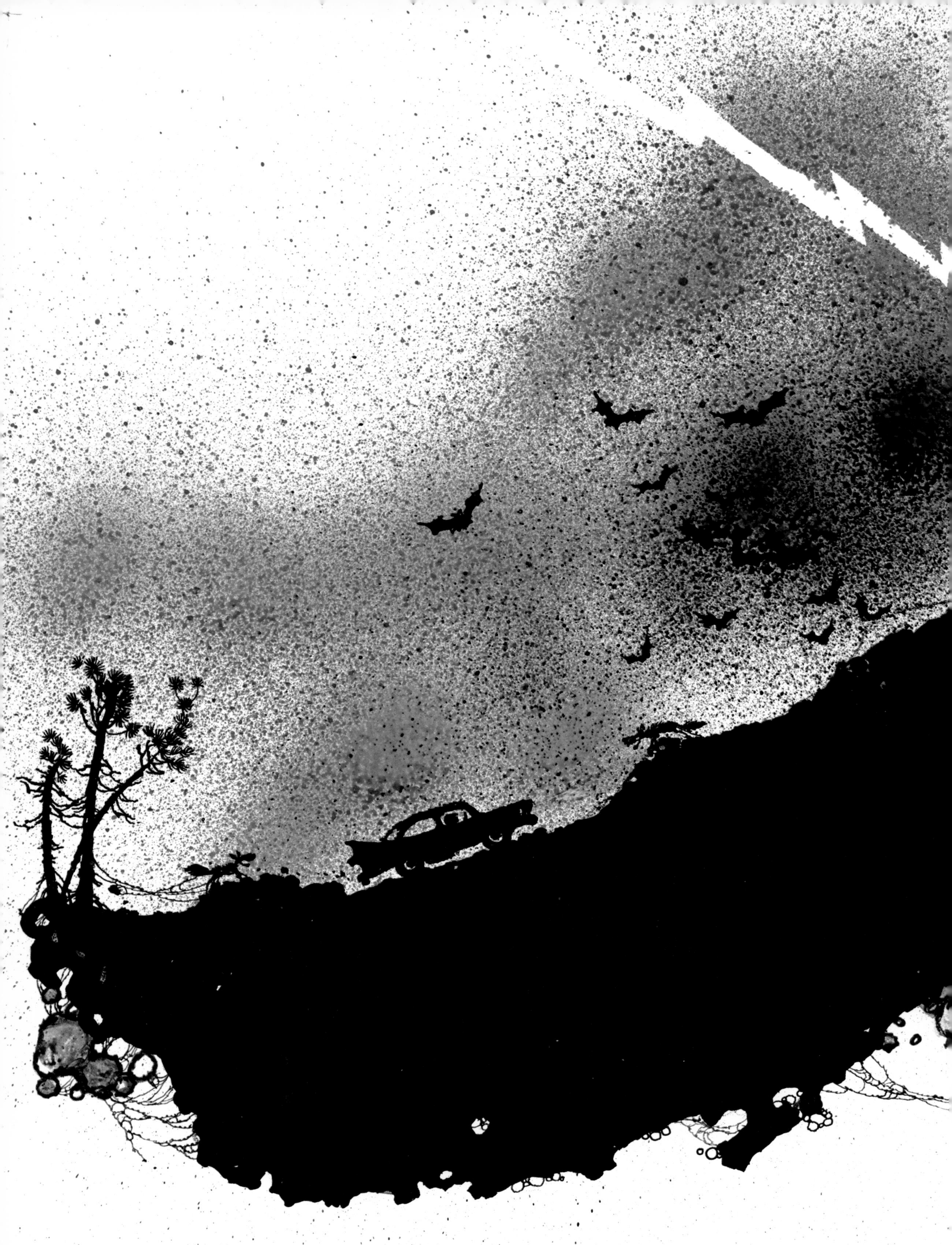

But one stormy night . . . a rich film producer arrived, looking for new blood for his horror films. He invited Dracula to become a big star in Hollywood.

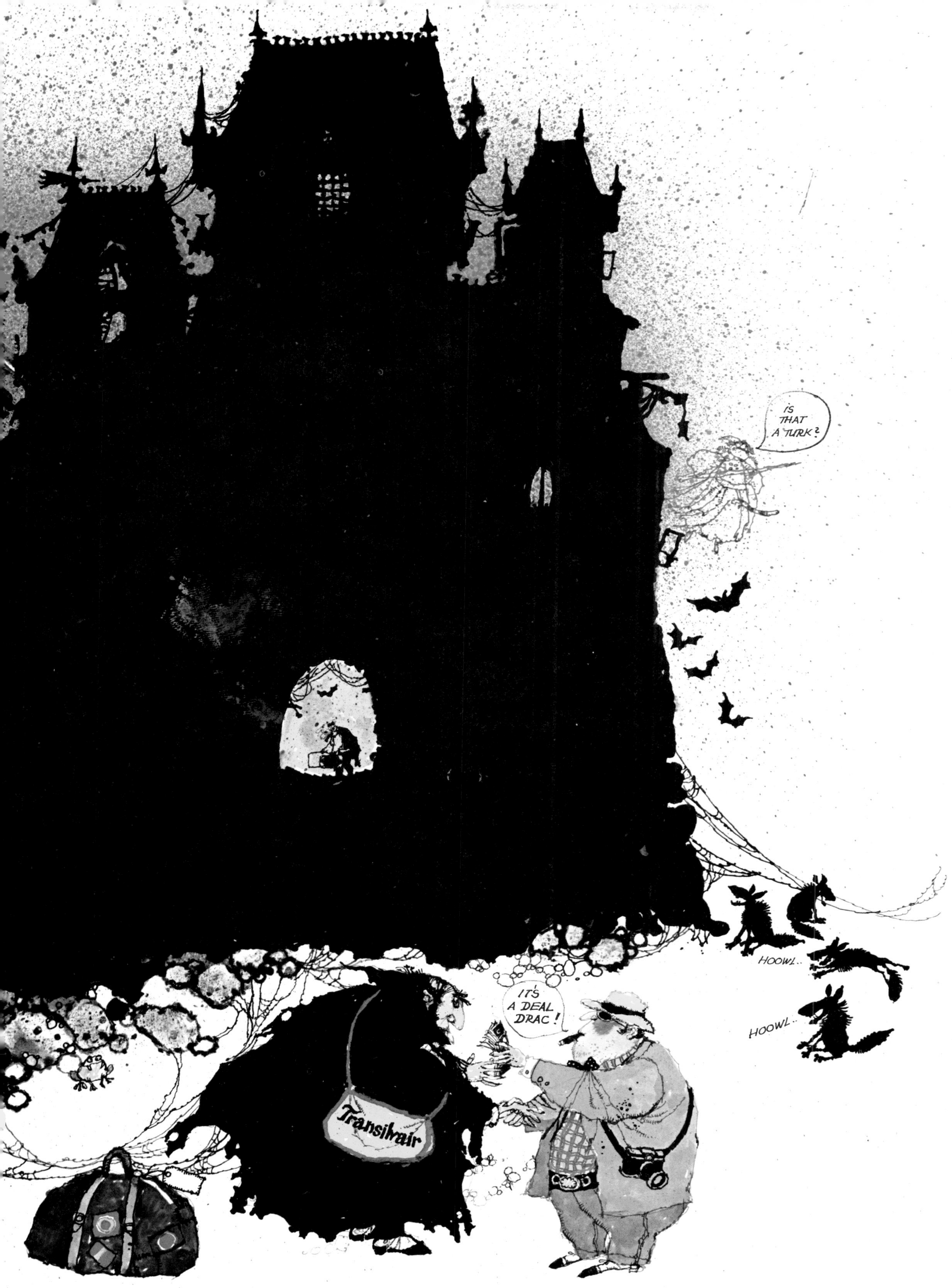
IS THAT A TURK?
IT'S A DEAL DRAC!
HOOWL..
HOOWL..
Transilvair

It was an offer he could not refuse, and he arrived in style on a magnificent Transylvair Jumbo prop-airliner.

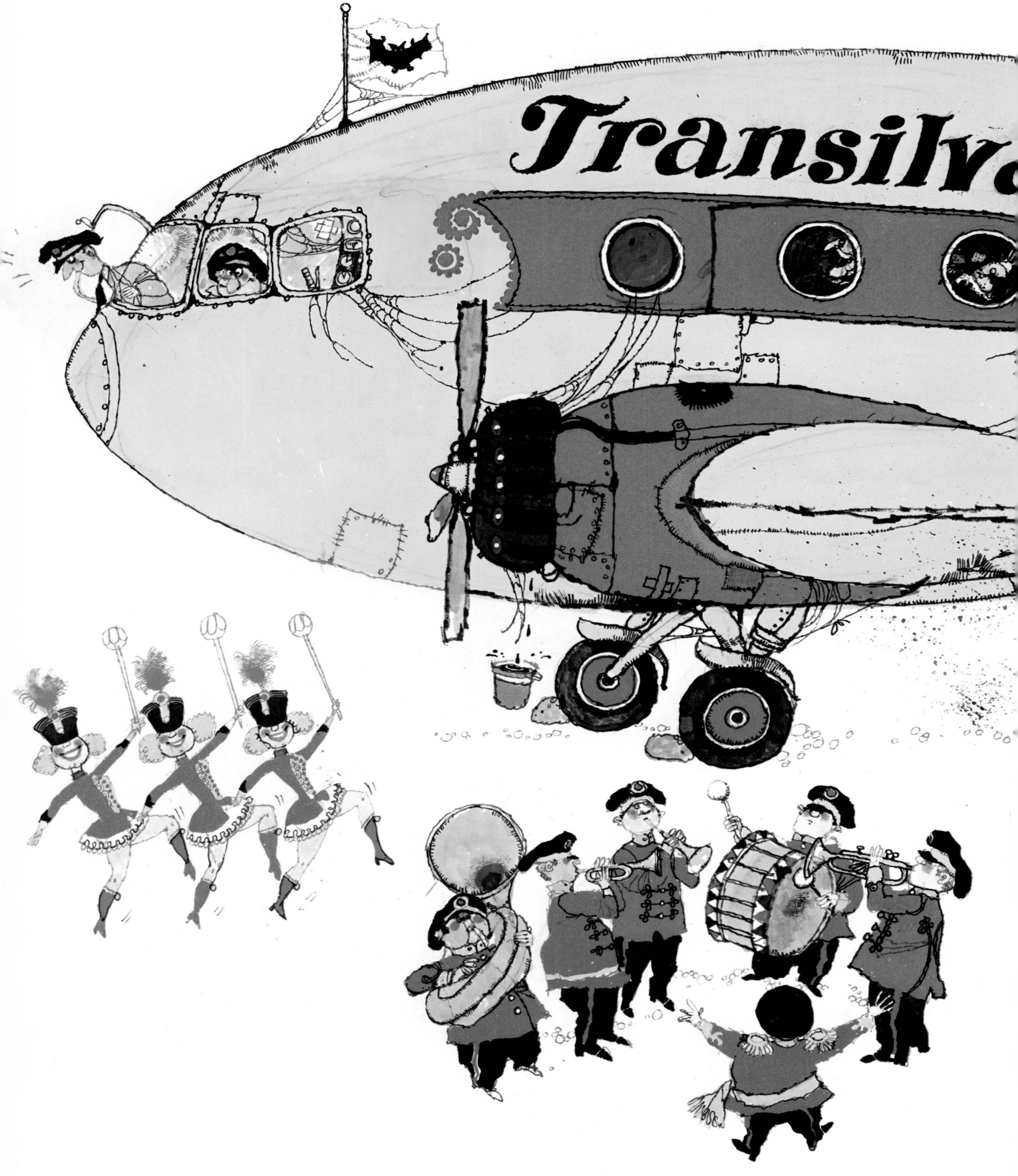
Transilva

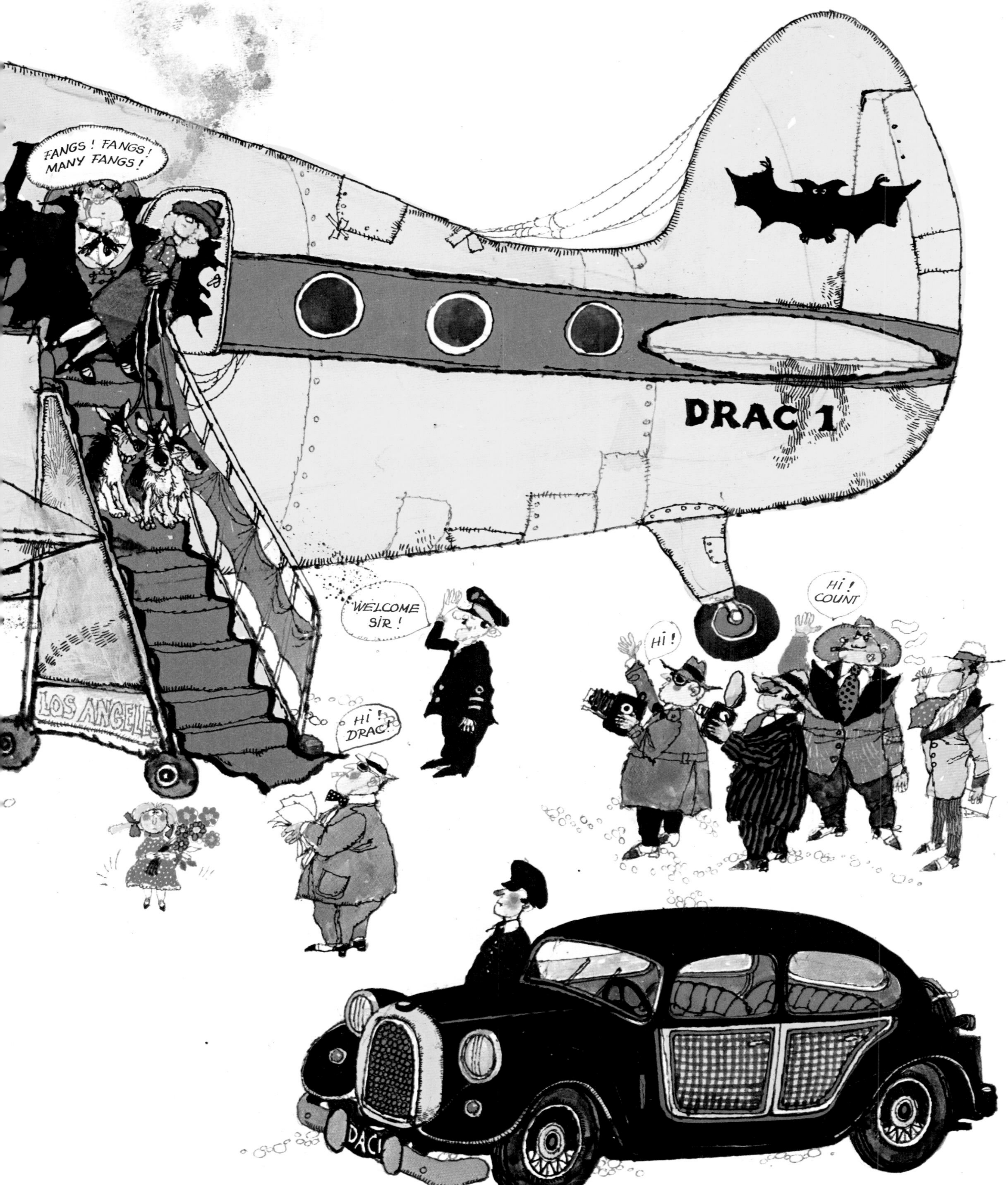
FANGS! FANGS! MANY FANGS!
DRAC 1
WELCOME SIR!
HI!
HI! COUNT
LOS ANGELES
HI! DRAC!
DAC1

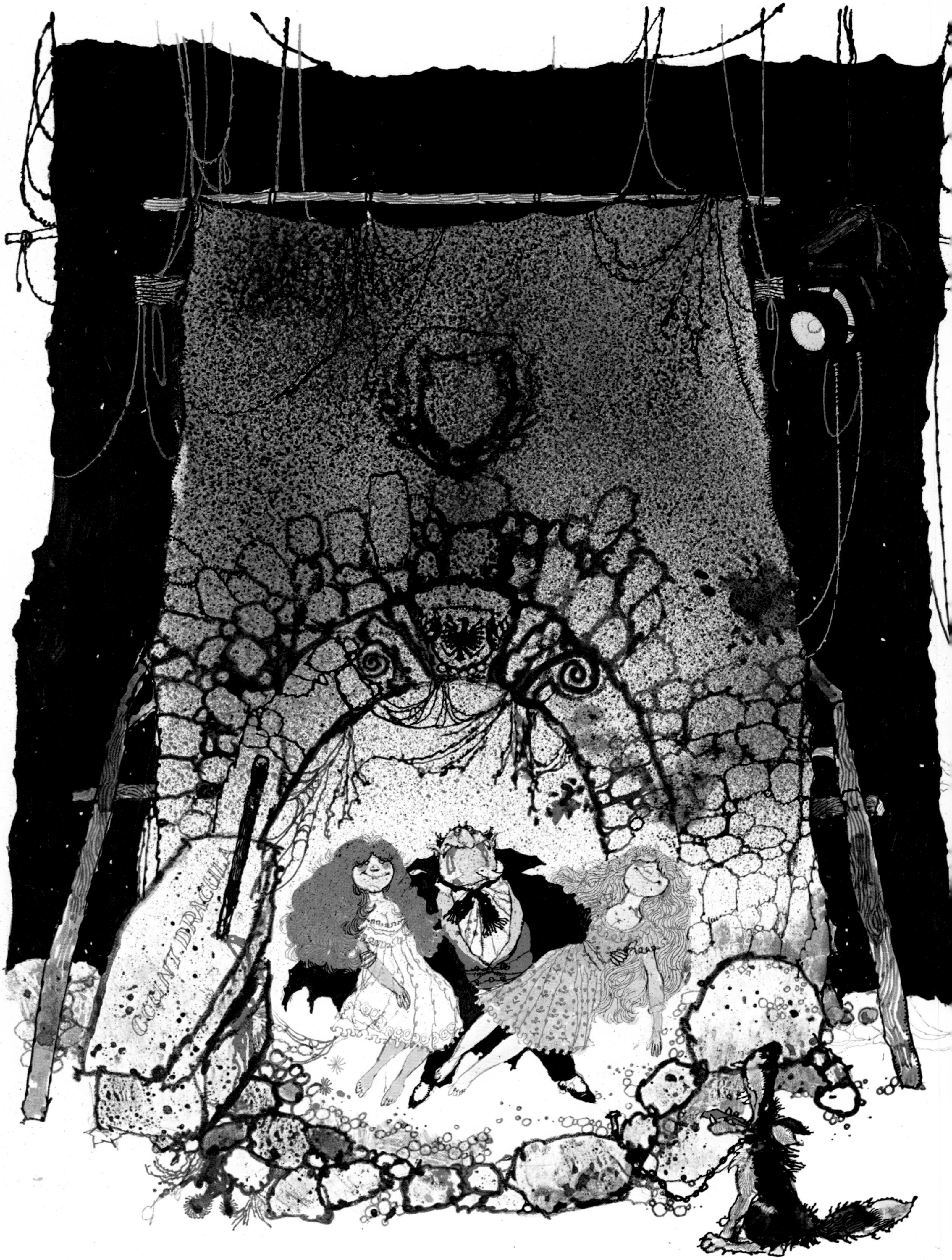
COUNT DRACULA

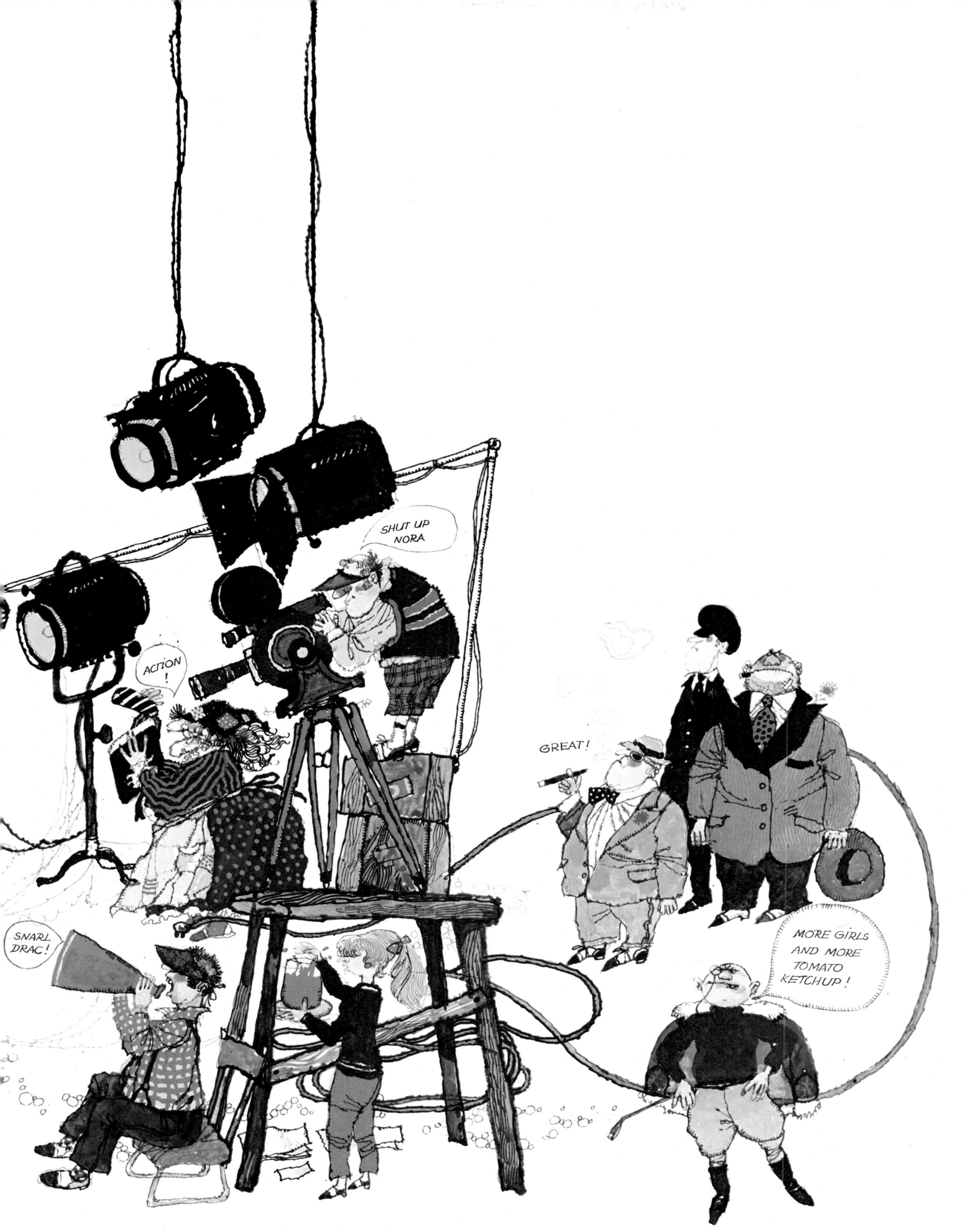
SHUT UP NORA
ACTION !
GREAT !
SNARL DRAC !
MORE GIRLS AND MORE TOMATO KETCHUP !

'Lights! Camera! Action!' said the Director. And Dracula was a star.

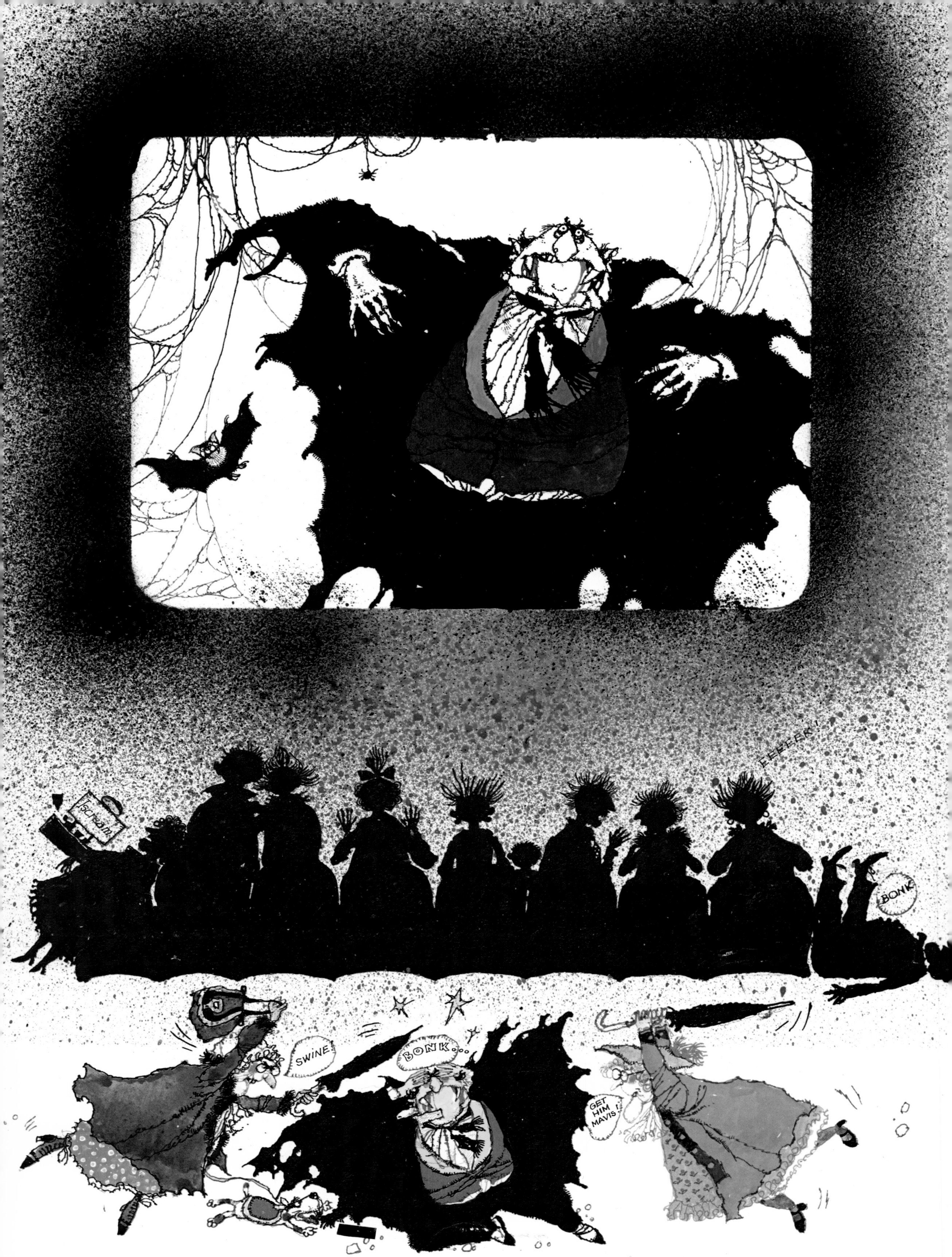
Iscream
EEEEEK!
BONK
SWINE!
BONK...
GET HIM MAVIS!

His films were a sensation, but he was frequently beaten up by dear old ladies.

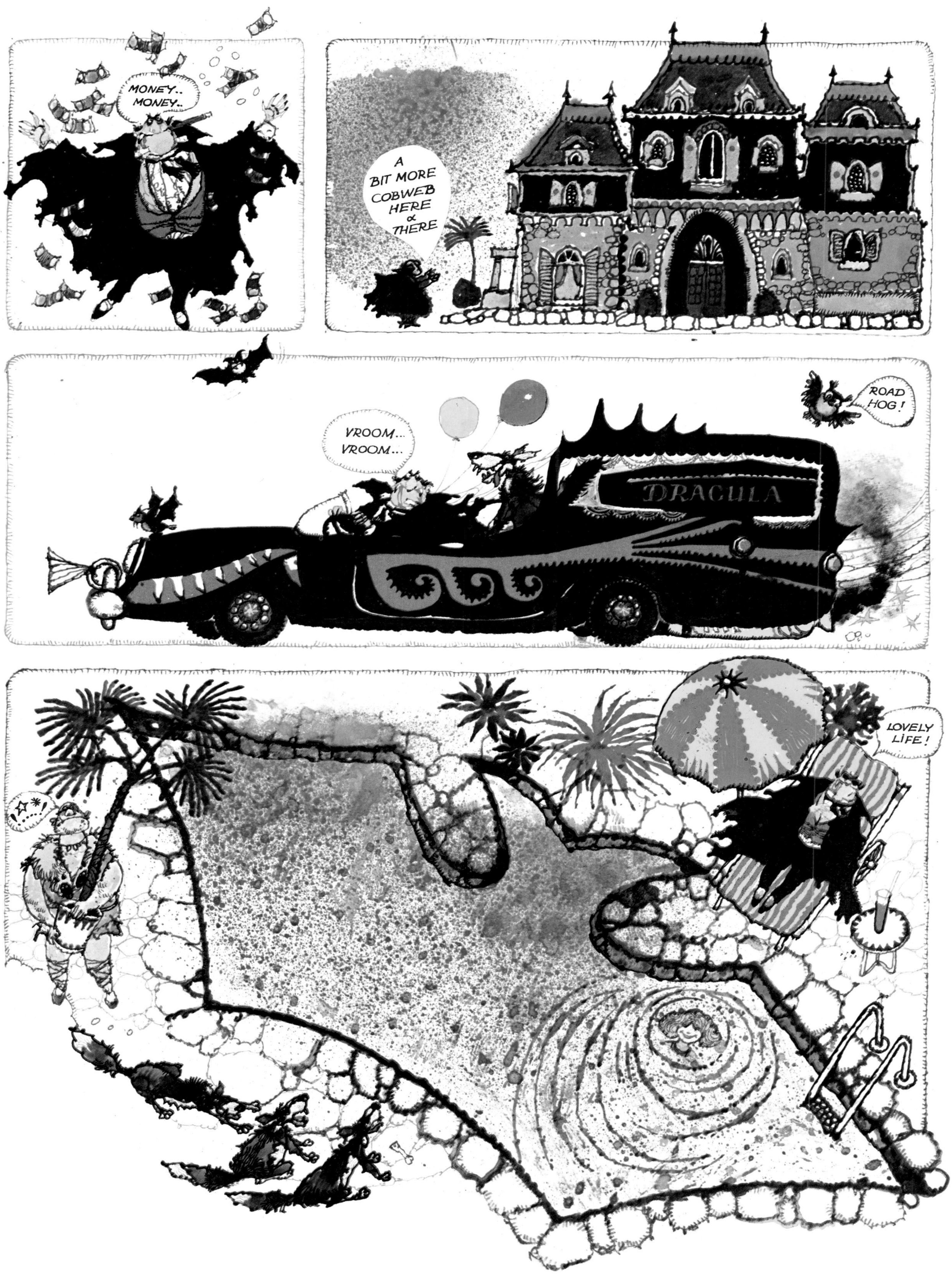
MONEY.. MONEY..
A BIT MORE COBWEB HERE & THERE
VROOM... VROOM...
ROAD HOG!
DRACULA
LOVELY LIFE!

He became very rich. He bought a new castle, a new car, and a bat-shaped swimming pool.

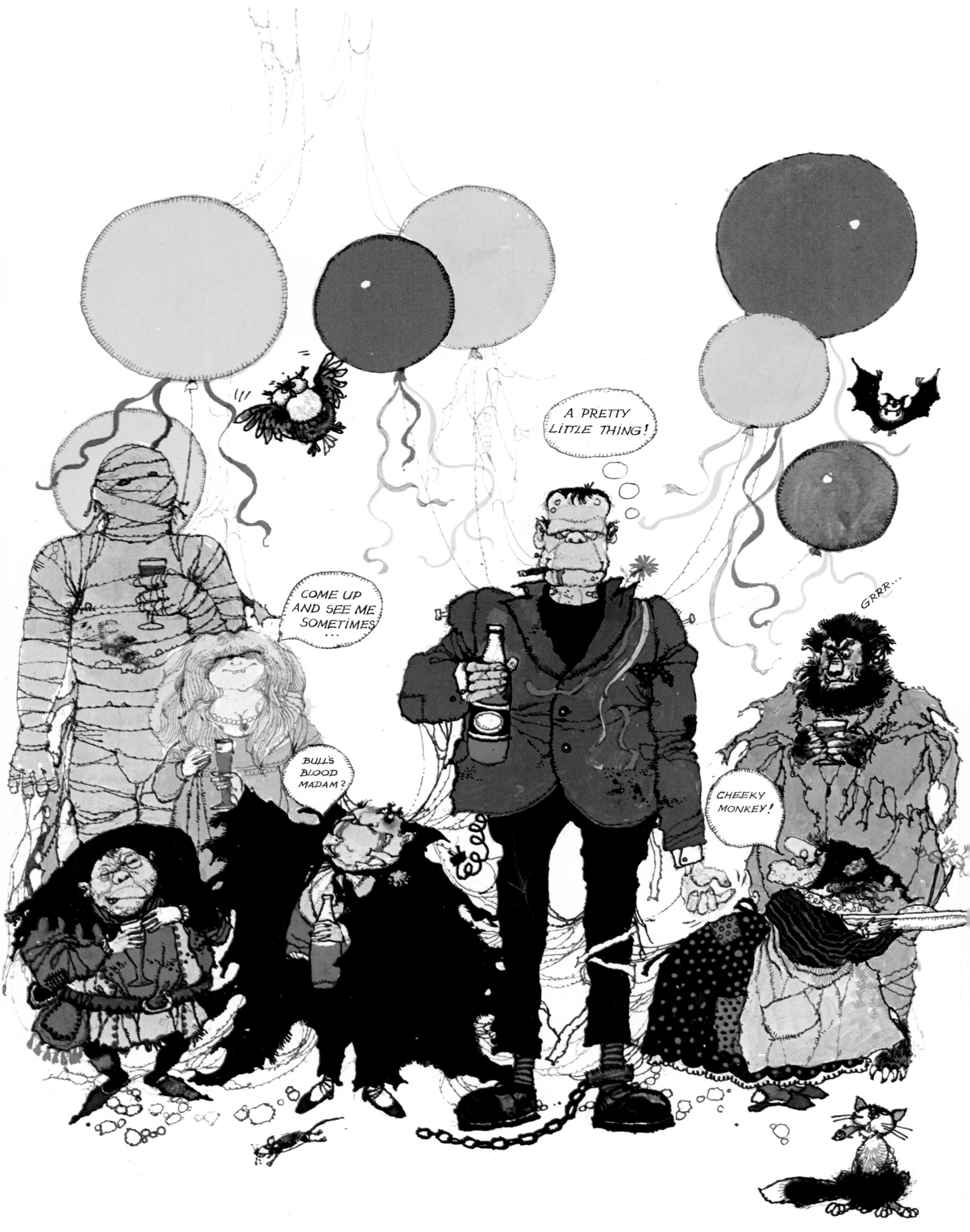
A PRETTY LITTLE THING!
COME UP AND SEE ME SOMETIMES ...
BULL'S BLOOD MADAM?
GRRR...
CHEEKY MONKEY!

He held monster parties for his fellow film-stars.

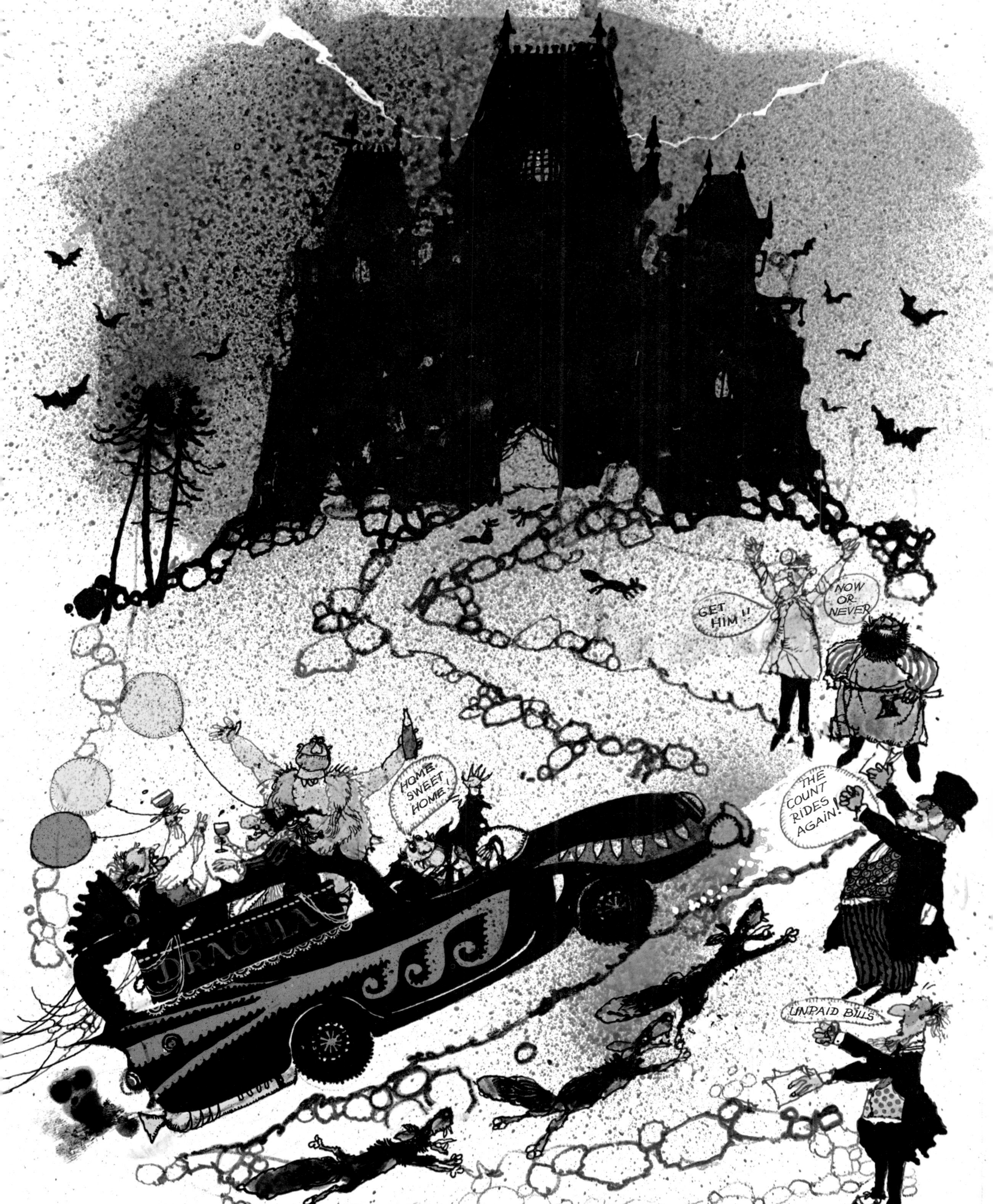
DRACULA
HOME SWEET HOME!
GET HIM!!
NOW OR NEVER
THE COUNT RIDES AGAIN!
UNPAID BILLS

But his heart belonged to Transylvania, and when he returned his old friends were waiting for him.

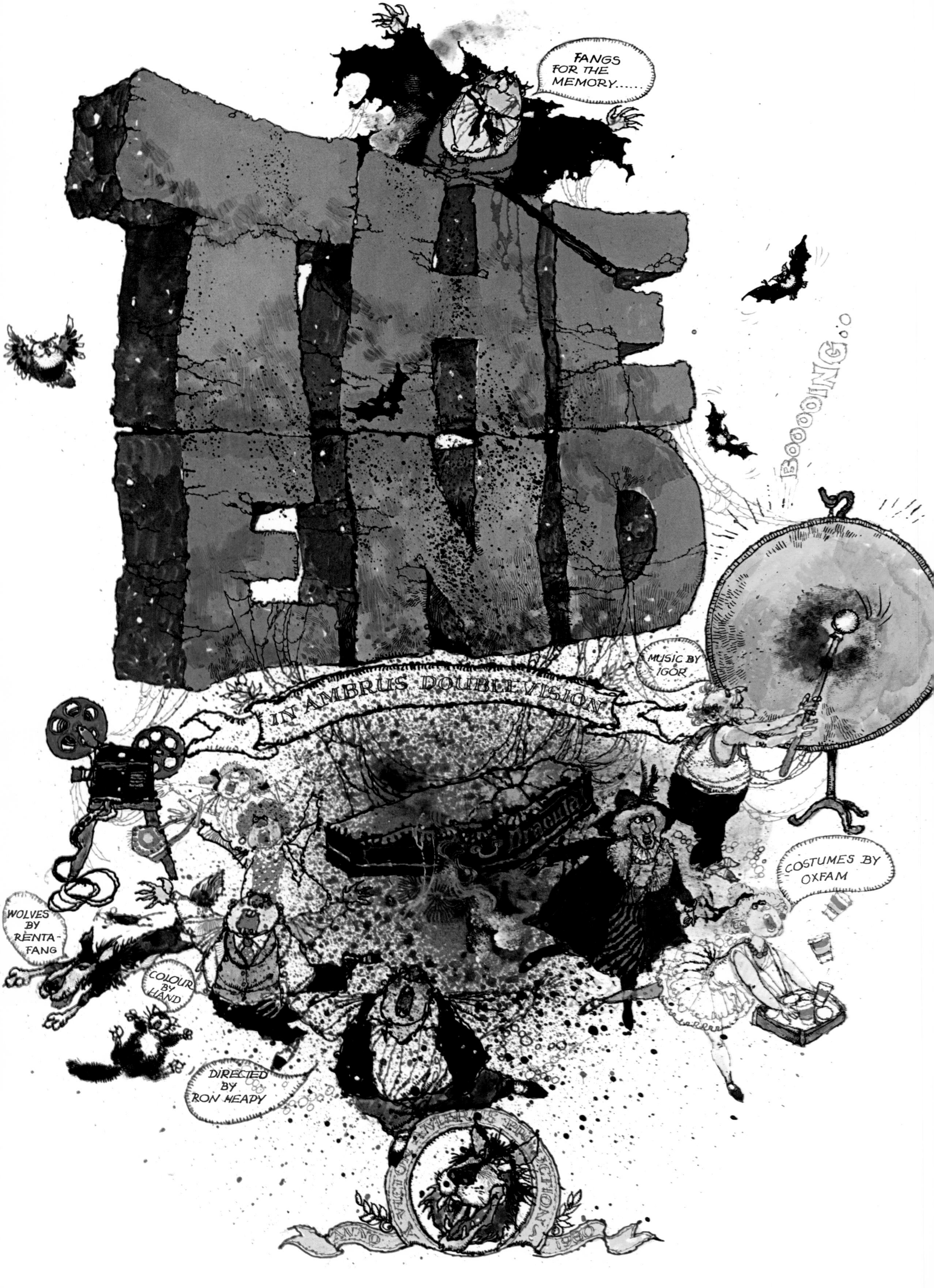
FANGS FOR THE MEMORY......
THE END
BOOOOING..
IN AMBRUS DOUBLE VISION
MUSIC BY IGOR
Dracula
COSTUMES BY OXFAM
WOLVES BY RENTA-FANG
COLOUR BY HAND
DIRECTED BY RON HEADY